Hell of a Ride

✦

A first person biography of the 'gutsy' test pilot, Richard G. 'Dick" Thomas, notorious for his bold, daring and dashing flight test escapades!

Cynda Thomas and Velvet Thomas

iUniverse, Inc.
New York   Bloomington

Hell of a Ride

A first person biography of the 'gutsy' test pilot, Richard G. 'Dick" Thomas, notorious for his bold, daring and dashing flight test escapades!

iUniverse books may be ordered through booksellers or by contacting:

iUniverse
1663 Liberty Drive
Bloomington, IN 47403
www.iuniverse.com
1-800-Authors (1-800-288-4677)

ISBN: 978-0-595-52878-3 (pbk)
ISBN: 978-0-595-62933-6 (ebk)

Printed in the United States of America

IUniverse rev. date: 10/24/2008

Table of Contents

ACKNOWLEDGEMENTS

Without the expertise and advice of the following people, this book would not have been possible. Although Dick had thousands of words written on legal yellow pads, confirmation by witnesses was quite necessary. These people provided details and crucial information in the development of this book either by written notes, interviews or informal conversations. However, even if your name has not been mentioned in this book, our deepest gratitude and most sincere appreciation is extended to all of you who took part. For without your efforts and contributions this chapter in aviation history would not have been possible. Thank you so much:

Henry "Hank" Chouteau- Retired Chief Pilot, Northrop; Mike Kennedy-Northrop; Don Murray-Northrop; Roy Martin-Chief Test Pilot, Northrop; Lee Philips-Northrop; George Sterling-Northrop; Bob Kaminski-Northrop; Carl Weyl-Northrop; John Cashen-Retired V.P., Northrop; Steve Smith-retired V.P.,Northrop; Andy Titiriga-Northrop; Bob Wulf-retired V.P., Northrop; Keith Benson-Northrop; Dale Felix-Retired Chief Pilot, Boeing-Wichita; Tom Gillespie- retired, Beech Aircraft test pilot & former roommate at Parks Aeronautical College; Peter Soule-Classmate from Parks Aeronautical College; R/ADM retired Roger Box- Classmate of USNTPS; R/ADM retired J.R."Smoke" Wilson-Classmate of USNTPS; John P. Lane-USNTPS; Carl Dubac-USNTPS; Donald Bowen-USNTPS; Ms.Wyn Adams, widow of Captain Richard Adams,USNTPS retired; Skip Hickey-Wright Patterson associate; Major Ruthie

Williamson-USAFR Interview; Major Dan Vanderhorst, fellow test pilot of Tacit Blue; Jim Conahan, official Air Force Artist; Rod Ross, Mayville School classmate; Albert Thomas, brother, Gordon Clifgard - Cover Photo.

Thanks go to the following: Northrop-Grumman Corporation; The Quiet Birdmen; The Society of Experimental Test Pilots (SETP); The Flight Test Historical Foundation; The City of Lancaster's Walk of Honor; The Boeing Company; and Michael Montgomery, Positive Image Photo-Graphics.

DISCLAIMER

Difficulty in writing a person's life that has often been controversial is a chore. We have tried to put Dick's words, taken from notepads, in the most exciting way to interest the reader. Certain names have been changed and other names have been left out to prevent any personal injury. However, all phases of the book are as truthful as could be verified and backed by actual documentation when necessary. In many cases, real names are referred to with love and admiration. The fictitious names were used to protect the writer and still explain the corrupt practices and abuse that went on in the corporate world.

THE PREFACE

This is the true story of Richard G. "Dick" Thomas, a New York State native, an Air Force pilot, a Kansas Air National Guard pilot, a Beech Aircraft production test pilot, and an experimental test pilot for the Boeing Airplane Company. His final flying employment was as an experimental test pilot for the Northrop Corporation, Edwards AFB, California.

This story brings to life a little boy's struggles to become the pilot he dreamed of being. He reminisces from his early childhood to his suffering from the crippling pallidotomy and Parkinson's disease. We have written it in first person using many of his writings and stories taken on tape.

From his humble beginnings in upstate New York, to his flying adventures at Edwards Air Force Base in California and secret locations, his story is unique and special. This book tells of an extraordinary life lived in an ordinary way. His flying experiences include over 8000 hours in 116 different aircraft flown by him during his career.

We have tried to capture the essence of our beloved man 'Dick'. In the following pages, his life unfolds as he often told his stories over the years.

During his extended illness with Parkinson's disease, Velvet (our youngest daughter) spent hours and hours with him taking notes of his childhood in Mayville, New York.

The horrific memories of the tragic pallidotomy, (that caused him to have a stroke and be left hemisphere denial, legally blind and unable to swallow) were my own (Cynda's) experience with Dick's operation. This reliving in the book brought back that nightmare; and inflamed me even more as I referred back to my notes taken that night in 2003.

CHAPTER 1

DEBILITY, DELIRIUM &
DREAMLAND

✦

Life was a hell-of-a ride, until my last gig just about did me in. I'm confined to this damned wheelchair, but it wasn't always like this. A thrill a minute is my story and I have to tell it because that's all I'm able to do now. Maybe it will save someone else from making the same mistake I did. You see, I said yes to the operation, and the doctor botched the pallidotomy on my brain surgery...

♦ ♦ ♦

As the white Lexus sped down Highland Avenue in San Bernardino toward St.Bernadine's Hospital, my wife, Cynda exclaimed, "We're lost, I can't find the hospital. I know this is a sign. I don't think the Lord wants us to go through with this!"

I answered, "I know where we are. We're in Cincinnati." Something was not right, but lately my mind had been playing tricks on me.

Was I doing the right thing in having this operation? Inside I felt sheer terror of what was waiting for me at the hospital…brain surgery. In all my years of testing airplanes, never had this feeling of doom spooked me before. Something was wrong here and I wasn't able to figure it out.

We wanted to be on our way to Wright-Patterson Air Force Base; where I was scheduled to give a presentation in front of my airplane, the Tacit Blue. There was to be a big celebration dinner with lots of fellow pilots giving accounts of their first flight in front of their airplanes in the museum. It was 2003, the 100th Anniversary of the Wright Brothers' first flight.

Dr. Iacono had promised me this pallidotomy would fix me 'right up'. The Parkinson's tremors in my hands would be less and my ablility to give my speech at the Air Force Museum much better. Those were just the words I wanted to hear. It was like giving candy to a kid, so I went for it. *Oh God, what have I done?*

As Cynda and I walked into the hospital, we could smell that awful antiseptic hospital odor, and I felt my knees weaken. This is wrong, I thought. *Why doesn't somebody stop me?*

So here we were in the hospital, both feeling railroaded into a situation that was unnerving to say the least. After check in and hospital preparations, Dr. Iacono came into pre-op and said in his salesmanship way, "Hey, Dick you're gonna do great."

I was to be the last operation of the day. He was doing three pallidotomies before me. Then he gave an order to the nurse and she gave me a couple of pills. The meds relaxed me and I went to sleep for awhile. Cynda stayed by my side the rest of the day.

At 4:00 p.m., the team of interns came and put me on the gurney to go to the operating room. It was my turn, I was awake and panic rose in my throat. Unable to speak, unable to react, I felt totally locked up and began to go through the motions like a robot. I saw the doctor approach me. Everything was blurry and hazy, as if there was a fog surrounding each person. What to do? I couldn't respond; I couldn't react. I remember the doctor talking to me, but what did he say?

I could hear myself telling him, "I don't want to do this, I've changed my mind".

Why couldn't he hear me? I tried to grab the railing on the wall as they pushed the gurney down the hall toward the operating room. We arrived at the operating room. The automatic doors swung open. I saw one nurse and Iacono's side-kick Felipe. It was too late; they transferred me to a strange looking table in a sitting position. *God no, I don't want to do this,* I looked for Cynda, but she had gone to the waiting room. Then the doctor became concerned about something and went to bring Cynda into the operating prep room.

Now we were in a room with a big dome-like apparatus above my head, this must be the CT scanner. Before me was a very large plate glass window and in front of that was the operation panel with buttons, levers and knobs. It extended approximately six to eight feet long and was about two to three feet deep. I saw Cynda leave that room, I didn't want her to go. But she left to go to the waiting room again. The doctor told her he would see her in about 20 minutes as that was all the longer this operation was supposed to take. I realized it was too late, I could not fight anymore. *Again, I silently cried out for help…* but still no voice. Cynda could not hear me.

Then suddenly I heard it; the shrill sound of the high powered drill. The doctor placed it to my skull near the top of my right forehead. I felt the push of the drill as it penetrated my skull; my scream was silenced as the pain was excruciating. I collapsed, the pain too intense, then in my comatose state…

◆   ◆   ◆

I hear the high-pitched whine of my F-5A jet engine going round in my head as my airplane continued to spin out of control. Something is amiss, I radio back to Edwards tower advising them I am about to leave the plane. Strange, their man radios me in a nonchalant way 'roger'. I repeat my radio message and give them my approximate fix, almost over Mt. Whitney. Then I hit the button and I am on my way out. The canopy flies off, and I feel the force of the ejection seat as it blasts me into space. The aircraft falls away. Bang! Suddenly something hits my helmet and knocks me out cold. When I come to, the automatic parachute is already open. Where to land? All I see are rocks the size of cars and larger. Nowhere to land, I prepare for a brutal boulder landing and get in the fetal position. I hit hard and my knees buckle, I pass out again.

Where am I? Oh God, I remember now, all I see are huge boulders and deep ravines. I look down over the rocks and see a little smoke below me and the remains of the aircraft. I am actually at a much higher altitude. It is very cold and I am shivering and my legs are hurting. I remember I have just ejected over Mt. Whitney and survived. It is November 4th, 1965.

I try to stand, and find my knees are bruised and sprained. It is difficult to stand, I am confused and disoriented. I sit again to get my bearings. What to do next, the automatic antenna on my helmet is broken so radioing my position is not possible. I know as soon as Edwards AFB tower control personnel alert the Northrop organization, Hank Chouteau will be looking for me. It isn't long before I see that wonderful sight of an F-5A coming towards me up the Owens Valley.

I shout, "Hey, here I am up here."

Hank is passing over the crash scene which is several thousand feet below me. He makes several more passes as I wave frantically, hoping he will see me. No good, he leaves me and heads back to the base at Edwards.

Searching through my flight suit I find only matches and a few pieces of maps. The weather on the valley floor is an unusual 70 degrees for November. But why don't I have more emergency equipment with me? What a joke on me, not even a flight jacket and it feels like about 40 degrees up here. A question I will always think about in the future. I decide to gather up my parachute and hike down closer to the crash. I am sure their search will be nearer the site. I stand and find my knees will hold me. Walking gingerly and dragging my chute, I struggle down a rather steep wash about 500 feet. At this point I stop and rest, I think of my three little ones at home and I pick up three small rocks, something to give them when I get home. I put them into the leg pocket of my flight suit and feel my matches. It occurs to me I can start a fire as well as spread out my parachute for the search plane.

Out of the south comes a C-120 piloted by another friend, Col. Jesse Jacobs from Edwards AFB. He passes over the crash scene. I wave and have my parachute stretched out for him to see. He doesn't see me as he is still a couple thousand feet or more below me. I grab the matches along with pieces of note paper and a map from my pockets, gather some brush near me and start a fire. He sees the smoke then sees me, waving his wings he heads south towards home base. I wonder what's next and only God knows. In a very short time I hear the whir of an H-21 helicopter. Boy, what a thrill that was to see…God, all I need now is a drink of water.

What has happened to me, I can't see and I can't swallow. My left side doesn't seem to be working right. I hear people talking around me, who are these people. I'm afraid, am I dead? Where's Cynda? Where are the kids? Oh God what is next? I want to sleep. Should I sleep? I'm sure I have a slight concussion. My head must have hit the canopy when I ejected. My forehead hurts so badly.

♦   ♦   ♦

The hospital nurses are wheeling me out of ICU. I can't remember why I am here. Is it because of the crash? Confusing the issue are strangers all around. Then I realize that I am 73 years old, not 35. What year is this? 2002? 2003? It comes back to me slowly; it is 2003, not 1965. I am in St. Bernadine's Hospital, but what has been done to me? The orderlies are taking me to a room and putting me in a bed. They are talking about me as if I'm not here and I worry about what they are saying. Here I am in a hospital bed and unable to speak. I don't know how long I have been here or what has happened to me. I guess it is the morning after the operation.

I heard a familiar voice, and Cynda came into the room. In a split second, she blurted out, "Oh my God, what has he done to you?"

Her question registered, but I was unable to speak. Then it dawns on me something must have gone wrong in surgery and my ability to speak and see has been terribly impaired. My left side is paralyzed and I heard her say, "Damn him, he's made you have a stroke and the left side of your face is drooping down."

Then she picked up my left hand and arm and it had no control or strength in it. She stormed out to the desk and I heard her yell at the nurse to see Dr. Iacono. The nurse made no response, but called on the telephone to someone, then told her the doctor was on his way. I could hear Cynda as she paced back and forth beside my bed, mumbling obscenities regarding the doctor; she was always like a cornered little Tasmanian devil when she got mad. And, was she boiling, I almost felt sorry for the doctor, I knew she was going to let him have it with both barrels!

As he stepped into the room, the fur began to fly and she exploded with, "What the hell have you done to my husband, you lying S.O.B", only she didn't abbreviate one word.

He backed off and put his hand up to ward off her attack saying, "Now Mrs. Thomas, Dick will come out of this, see he is just fine," and he ran his thumb nail up the bottom of my right foot, which was sticking out of the sheet.

Then she asked, "Why can't he see or swallow?" It was then that I knew things had gone terribly wrong in the surgery.

For the rest of the day, she stayed by my side trying to feed me 'gluck' as she called it, thickened water and juice. Whatever it was, I couldn't swallow it. I was dehydrated then and became worse during the day. I was very miserable; and the doctor ordered physical therapy for me. Was he out of his head, I couldn't even eat or see and he wanted me to try to get up and walk!

Exhausted, weak and depressed, I retreated into a deep sleep. Then I heard the nurse asking where Richard Thomas' medication book might be, the nurse was calling, "Richard wake up for your medicine, come on Richard wake up."

◆   ◆   ◆

Richard, I thought, who calls me Richard? I go by Dick Thomas; only in my home town, Mayville, do they call me Richard. My home town, can I get there from here, maybe everything will be okay if I can go home to Mayville, my address I recall, 71 Valley Street, Mayville, Chautauqua County, New York. It runs through my head over and over again until I loose consciousness.

Chautauqua County, Chautauqua County, Chautauqua, New York…I can hear Mom's words telling me, "Richard you were born April 2, 1930, on Howard Hill in the town of Chautauqua, New York. You are a lucky little boy because you have two older brothers, Donald and Freddie. They are four and two. They will take care of you like big brothers should."

Well I guess they did, as time passed my brother Donald Albert became my guardian angel. 'Cause in 1934, our Mom and Dad both worked during the great depression. They had to take any work they could get even if that meant leaving their little boys to care for themselves at home. It was a fact of life.

Often we found ourselves home alone with very little to eat, but since Albert was the oldest, he was the boss. The three of us were making dinner for ourselves one night. It was going to be liver; that was all we had. Albert was only eight, Freddie was six and I was four. Albert got a chair and a pan, pushed the chair to the stove, and put the liver in the pan. Then he stood on the chair and put the pan on the burner. The liver started to cook; it smelled awful. Albert was standing on the chair and said "Look the liver is burning. We better get it out of the pan."

But it was too late. We put the burned liver on a plate; knowing we had to eat it anyway as there was nothing else to eat in the house. We sat and looked at the liver, and then we began to eat it slowly. I took too big a bite, it tasted awful and I gagged on it. I tried hard to choke it down anyway but I could not swallow it. I tried to spit it out. Then, Albert looked at me and knew I was in trouble. I was choking. He jumped and grabbed me by the ankles and turned me upside down. I immediately coughed and spit up the liver. We both just sat there stunned, I stared at him and knew he had kept me from choking to death, quite a realization for a little guy. I decided I was not hungry and went off to bed. At four years old I knew how to put myself to bed.

◆   ◆   ◆

My eyes opened, the room was dark. My tongue was swollen and it felt like I had a mouth full of cotton; I couldn't swallow. What was wrong with my throat? I was starving, why couldn't I have something to eat. Why didn't someone help me? Where was Cynda?

I tried to find familiar things around me. I heard a nurse and saw a faint light but everything was blurry, I tried to yell, "Hey, can someone help me?"

I heard my own voice, but my words sounded funny and slurred. Then footsteps approached my bed and a light came on near by. "Mr. Thomas, can I get you something?" the nurse asked.

In my garbled way, I told her, "I need water."

She tried to give me a drink, but I strangled and choked convulsively. She rang for the head nurse who came running to help. Together they swabbed my mouth with wet sponges and gave me an injection to help me sleep through the rest of the night.

I laid there thinking *I'm in a heck of a jam and I need to be getting ready for my next test flight in the airplane. They will be expecting me at the field early in the morning. Slowly, I drifted off again.*

•   •   •

The field, the field, oh yeah, the baseball field, we looked forward to Sundays because after we finished our work around the house, Dad would take all of us to the ball field. He loved to play the game of baseball, and played quite well. He never made it to the minors but played every Sunday. His hope was that one of his boys would love the ballpark as much as he did. We all learned to love baseball. When Dad played any game baseball or golf, he played it the best he could. He was an avid fan of Babe Ruth, who was popular at the time, and told us boys regularly he wanted us to be able to hit like 'the Babe'. We got a baseball autographed by 'the Babe' himself. Aunt Ruth, Mom's sister, did lots of traveling. So, when she went to New York to see the series she managed to get a baseball autographed by 'Babe Ruth' just for us boys. We didn't really understand he was famous; gosh he was just a guy playing baseball like our Dad. We had heard Dad talk about him, so we were glad to get a baseball. Like kids do, we played with that ball at home until the cover came off.

You know, there was something I loved even more than baseball though. I couldn't get near them, but every time one flew overhead, I was mesmerized. Then one Sunday when Dad was playing ball, I got the chance of a lifetime. I saw a bright red airplane doing circles and loops overhead. I watched intently as the old barnstormer came in for a landing, then taxied right up to the outfield and cut his engines.

He jumped out and yelled "Free rides for kids" I ran to Dad and asked if I could go up.

He gruffly answered, "No, you are not going up in one of those flying machines."

I was crushed. But over his shoulder I heard my Mom's kind voice say, "Yes, Richard, you may go, but only if you take both of your brothers with you."

Dad said nothing. So, the three of us ran over to the pilot and watched as he wiped his airplane down a bit. He was wearing these special clothes. His pants were tight and tucked into leather boots that came up to his knees. He had a brown leather jacket with an eagle sewn on the sleeve. His helmet was brown leather too with a buckle under his chin and big black goggles were pushed on top of his head. A long white silky scarf was wrapped around his neck.

He looked very important to me. Then he asked "Well boys would you like to go up?"

We all three shook our heads yes. "Well, climb in." was just what we wanted to hear him say.

When we got into the seat, it felt too tight for all three of us. I couldn't really see out that good, but I was too excited to care. The pilot spun the prop a little; he jumped up on the side and leaned into the cockpit, pulled the choke out a little more, ran back and gave it a hefty spin, the propeller caught and the engine sputtered. He quickly climbed into the cockpit, gave it a little more power and the plane rumbled down the baseball outfield through the grass. Finally it taxied out to the dirt road and began to gain speed. Suddenly I felt the plane lift off the ground. I could barely see out so I stood on my tiptoes. But, when the pilot banked the airplane I saw everything getting smaller and smaller.

Like many young boys, I had dreamed of this moment and now my dream was coming true. That ride turned out to be the greatest pleasure I had ever had and from that point on I knew my destiny. I was hooked. I wanted to be a pilot. I never told anyone, but kept it my secret dream. Dad believed in hard work for us boys, not frivolousness. And flying, that was just a silly new adventure to him. That was March 1935.

◆　　　　◆　　　　◆

For the next few days my head was in and out of the clouds. Sometimes I knew where I was and sometimes I believed I was back in time. Would this hell I was experiencing ever pass? Then one morning I woke up to the real world and began to realize what really had taken place. It wasn't easy to function with my eyesight so impaired. In fact, I could only see a span for about 12 inches to the right. Swallowing thickened water wasn't even possible. And the starvation I was experiencing was so painful; my agonizing groans frustrated Cynda to tears. No instructions were given by the doctor to the hospital for my recovery and each day became another wretched nightmare. Cynda's threatening declarations to the doctor and the hospital finally got me some attention. And after ten days, I was transferred to the Ballard Rehabilitation Hospital in San Bernardino.

Those next few weeks turned into months and after coming home in August, I realized I wasn't going to have much of a life from there on. My daughter, Velvet, came several evenings a week after teaching school all day. She asked questions and took notes about my life as a kid. We had a great father-daughter relationship. I was at least coherent by this time. And as I reminisced about those early years, it brought back memories of my childhood often forgotten.

CHAPTER 2

THE EARLY YEARS

✦

By the summer of 1935, we had moved from Buffalo to Fredonia, New York and from there to Hartfield. Dad had a job in a restaurant and Mom was teaching school. With the money she made from teaching, she bought herself a brand new Model T. But one night it was stolen right out of the driveway beside our house. Dad said if he'd been driving it, it wouldn't have been stolen 'cause he'd have left the gas tank empty. We moved around a lot as Dad was not happy with the jobs he was able to get. Albert and Freddie both started school in Dunkirk and Fredonia, and then we moved back to Buffalo. We lived in two rooms in a tenement house. My two brothers and I slept in the big room which left the tiny bedroom for Mom and Dad.

The fall of 1936 was a big year for me; I was starting school in Buffalo. I was able to tag along with my older brothers and be one of the guys. I could hardly wait for school to start. Mom was teaching me to read and print my letters. Mom said I was coming along nicely; I could read well in the first grade. My teacher at school was very pretty and I did everything she told me to do. I loved getting up early and eating Mom's homemade cinnamon rolls or pancakes for breakfast. We had real maple syrup for our pancakes tapped from trees all around the local area.

The folks decided to move again and were making plans to get their own store in Hartfield. But that didn't work out and back they moved to Fredonia. It seemed like we moved every year or sometimes twice a year. Times were very tough then and we did without just like a lot of other kids our age.

By now it was early 1938. I was almost finished with the second grade. I was rapidly approaching my eighth birthday in early April, without any events or catastrophes. But one morning I woke feeling very ill. I called Mom and when she examined me she knew I was a very sick little boy. She called Dr. Reynolds from Beemis Point to come to the house. He took my temperature and listened to my heart. Then after examining me, the two of them talked outside my room. Mom came back into my room and broke the news to me, "Richard, the doctor says you have rheumatic fever. You will not be able to go to school and you must stay in bed until you are well."

Mom was such a good nurse that I completely recovered by the end of school. Our school would be out at the end of May and only a couple of weeks were left. Finally, I was allowed to go back to school. The three of us boys rode the bus to school and back. But going home, I had to ride it all the way until it came back around; because it couldn't stop going down hill. Usually the bus stopped at the bottom of the hill, Albert and Freddie got off and walked back up the hill to our home, but I was still too weak. After the kids all got off, and the bus was coming back, he could stop going up the hill and let me off in front of my house. I have to say it was a very steep hill, one that was fun to ski down in winter too.

My brothers and I had a wonderful time that summer. It was an idyllic time in upstate New York. Dad continued to take us to the ball field. But, the three of us had found a new love. We had discovered model airplanes and started building them with balsa wood and rice paper. Aunt Ruth would buy us little engines to put in them and we started learning to fly them on the big field near our house. There was a little room or closet with a window near the top of the stairs and Mom gave us the room for building our flying machines. We spent every minute after chores in that little room figuring out how our little creations went together and what made them fly.

There were a few other fun things we found to do too. We spent many hours in Dad's old boat fishing. The three of us used to drag the crusty thing out on Chautauqua Lake whenever we could con him into letting us use it. The night before we went fishing we laid out on the damp grass and shined the flashlight on the ground, those night crawlers were big fat juicy worms and the fish liked them. As I remember back we spent some time bailing water out of the boat with a big can. We weren't too concerned about it.

Then, one day Albert told Dad, "That old boat has a leak."

Dad just replied, "Well when you go out on the lake, the wood will swell when it gets wet, when that happens, it will seal itself and she won't sink." Dad gave the old boat a new coat of paint every summer. The boat finally rotted, but it never did sink, thank goodness.

Luckily, Dad got a job as Manager of the A & P Stores in Mayville. So I started school there in the third grade. Then Dad was able to buy the Red & White Store in Mayville. The folks wanted to send us boys to college so we would have a much better life. Mom had her teacher's certificate and she told us how important it was to have an education if you wanted to succeed in life, even if you wanted to fly airplanes! So Albert started keeping me informed about all the classes I would have to take if I really wanted to be a pilot. All of us really wanted to fly, but it seemed a far-fetched idea. We talked about it to Mom, but we knew better than to talk about it to Dad. He only believed in one thing, hard work. And he made sure his boys developed the same value.

During the winter months we seemed to have even more chores to do when the lake froze over. People bought and stored big chunks of ice for the summer months. There were ice companies that had huge warehouses for storing ice for those hot months. They had bales of straw lining the inside walls of their sheds and their ice blocks could weigh as much as two hundred pounds. During the summer Dad had us working at delivering ice to people around the lake.

The ice could freeze to a foot thick in winter. Many people thought they could drive their cars across the frozen lake; but some of the time the ice would break and the cars would fall into the lake. I remember it happened at least once every winter. The Lake Authority finally started to police the area to cut down on the cars trying to drive across on the ice.

It was soon to be Thanksgiving and then Christmas. There was always a lot of snow in our area and most of the kids had skis. Mayville was built on a very hilly area around Lake Chautauqua. Some of the streets were very steep, with hills two hundred feet high. The boys would hike up to the top of the hill, put the leather strap over their boots and slide down. I had seen some of the older kids do it. It looked like a lot of fun. Dad was making the three of us skis for Christmas. He would soak the maple planks in hot water then bend the ends of the planks around the iron bedstead and tie them. After they dried curled, he would wax them so the moisture of the snow would not penetrate the ski, and it would slide easily. Even though I was very young, I was sure I could do it. It would almost feel like flying.

Christmas morning came, we didn't have a tree, but we each had a red knit stocking with some maple sugar candy in it. Aunt Dee would make the candy from the sap that came from the maple trees near our house. We each got a box at Christmas time. Dad handed Albert, Freddie and me, each a large package wrapped in newspaper and tied with string. We knew what was inside; we had watched Dad work on those skis for the whole month. After tearing those packages open, I ran to the hallway to get my lace-up boots and put them on. I slid my feet through the leather straps that held the skis on my feet. I couldn't wait to ski. A foot of snow covered the ground for weeks and as luck would have it, new snow covered everything with a light dusting during the night. Mom looked at me and knew what I was thinking, she said, "Breakfast first Richard and then skiing". She was right and always corrected me with that soft love; it was easy to do what she asked.

I remember that day I learned to ski. No one taught me and no one gave me any instructions. I just climbed to the top of the hill and slid my feet into those straps, pointed my skis downhill and away I went. I fell several times. But it was mostly a day of fun. I played all that day with my brothers until the sun went down and it began to get really cold. We got our things together and went home, as tomorrow was Sunday and we knew we all were expected to work. It had been a special Saturday because it was Christmas, but normally Dad didn't let us do such things as to have the whole day off. We were thankful to Dad for the great day of fun we had had due to his hard work and efforts to make our skis.

Sunday morning came and Dad woke us all up at seven o'clock. He told us we had to shovel snow as it had snowed again that night. We had to carry canned goods down to the cellar because Mom had canned all day on Christmas Day. Our next job was pitching hay in the barn. Mom had a horse named Lady. It was too cold for Lady to go to the snow covered pasture. We boys got dressed and went to the kitchen for Mom's breakfast of pancakes and maple syrup. We drank hot coffee as it would help keep us warm outside.

The three of us bundled up and began shoveling snow, when Dad wasn't watching we had an impromptu snowball fight. Once that job was over, we went to the kitchen to carry Mom's preserves down to the cellar. Dad had killed a deer a few days before and we helped him put the meat in the cellar too. After lunch, we trailed off to the barn to tend to Lady. At last, finished with chores, we flopped down in the hay and talked about flying machines again.

I asked Albert, "What kind of plane do you want to fly?"

"I don't know," he answered, "I guess a real fast one, so I can do loops and spins and all kinds of tricks and acrobatics."

"Wow, I want to do that too!" was my response as I thought of it dreamily.

Then we heard Dad's voice. He brought us back to reality, calling us to dinner. We hushed quickly since we didn't talk about flying in front of Dad.

So this is how we spent most of the winter. We worked hard doing a lot of physical exercise as we dreamed of flying airplanes. Spring was approaching and that meant baseball season again. I looked forward to baseball, not so much because of the game. Oh yeah, I liked it enough, but I was hoping for another chance encounter with one of those 'barnstormers' as Dad called them. It was almost April when I would be another year older.

That summer was pretty uneventful. Many hours were spent down at the lake and when I wasn't building model airplanes with my brothers, I was learning to ride a bike. Big Little Books were the thing then and we had lots of them. They were all about super heroes and I liked reading them as much as possible. Money saved from my part of our shared paper route would be spent at the Five and Dime Store. Since we all worked the paper route, we shared the profit.

Sometimes we would buy these books by the dozen. They cost us 5 cents each. But my favorite Big Little Book was "Dick Tracy". He had all kinds of adventures and was able to get out of any kind of trouble. Dick Tracy was my favorite character too, because as the best super hero of them all, he seemed to be the most realistic, always ready to help people.

The end of summer was coming and one day the three of us were playing baseball. We had our 'Babe Ruth' ball and Albert was pitching, Freddie was up to bat and I was the catcher. Well, Albert threw the ball and Freddie swung and missed, the ball bounced out into the street and I ran after it. I didn't look and it was too late. I heard the car screech. It hit me on my left side and hooked onto my overalls. It dragged me all the way down the hill before it finally stopped.

Both of my brothers came running down the hill shouting, "Richard, Richard! Are you okay?"

Albert cried. I lay there crying and moaning, unable to speak, while Freddie ran to the house to get mother. Mom came running down the hill and tried to talk to me. I couldn't answer. She and my two brothers picked me up and carried me to our house. The people were very sorry and apologized, but said I ran right out in front of them. That was true, I had been thinking about our 'Babe Ruth' baseball.

Mom and Dad didn't take me to the doctor as we didn't have enough money. Mom seemed to think that I was okay. Nevertheless, I had to stay in bed for the next three weeks. As it turned out, I had a few cracked ribs but other than that I was okay. After that Mom kept a closer eye on me. But, I stayed in bed reading those comics and kept thinking that I wanted to be like Dick Tracy. Everyone said I was very lucky, because if the car had not caught onto my overalls I would have been squashed under the tire. Many neighborhood friends came to visit me. I was the center of attention. It was nice to feel special, but I wanted to get back to normal. After a month I felt better and we played baseball with that ball until the signature wore off and eventually the cover came off too. We never were able to hit like the 'Babe'.

During my time of recuperating, I began working on my own first model airplane. We three boys had always shared the building of our planes, this one was going to be special, and all mine. The three of us built many different model airplanes. We used every minute of spare time dad would allow. Some planes had wing spans of three feet and when we would crash one or two, we would have to rebuild them.

Well summer was almost over and school would start soon. It was time for me to resume my responsibility with my brothers on the paper route. Besides, I needed money for more plane supplies and comics. Dad never let me forget that everyone had to do his share and pull his own weight in this family. I knew that to be true.

CHAPTER 3

THE WAR YEARS

✦

The war in Europe was going full scale in 1939. Franklin D. Roosevelt, our president, was making all kinds of promises; but Mom and Dad didn't like the sound of things. With three boys they worried that their sons would get caught up in all the hype of the war. Sunday nights were spent listening to President Roosevelt on the radio. We talked about what a great man he was, and what a great country we lived in. He promised to do much for the Americans. Little did we know how serious that war would become.

My third grade year, I only focused on my schoolwork and one other thing. Aunt Dee had promised to take my cousin, Andy, and me to the World's Fair in New York. My health was back to normal and I was delivering papers again with my brothers. I saved all my money for the impending trip to the fair. It was rumored to be the gathering place for many barnstorming pilots; and I wasn't about to miss out on another plane ride. I dreamed of going up again. It was all I could think about.

Mom was aware of my flying desires and told me to start saving my money for college. I listened to her and gave up my weekly splurge on comic books and saved my few dimes for my future. She made sure we understood that education and good grades were important. Mom had struggled with Dad long enough to know she didn't want her sons to be limited by a lack of education. During the depression, the folks had been forced to work in numerous and sundry professions not always to their liking. Now they were able to secure their own store. The business was starting to make a little money and we were saving for a house of our own.

Mom had her eye on just the place. It was 59 Valley Street in Mayville. The people that owned the house were not ready to sell yet. But Mom would wait them out. It was a two-story house with a cellar, four big bedrooms and an attached apartment that could be rented out. The big two-story house sat on twelve acres right next to a ball field and within walking distance to Chautauqua Lake. This was her ideal house and she intended to have it someday.

Finally the time came to go to the fair, it seemed like I had waited forever. I was so excited because I knew I was going to get to see those barnstormers again. The three of us left in Aunt Dee's old Packard, me and my cousin Andy with Aunt Dee driving. Going to New York to the World's Fair didn't happen for many kids in my town and it sure was a huge treat for me.

As we arrived near the fairgrounds, we began to see lots of people standing around. Then I saw what I had been waiting to see for so long, planes of all colors, black shiny ones, red ones and yellow ones. The pilots were just as colorful with their fancy flying suits, boots and scarves. They were promoting some kind of stunt show and my Aunt stopped and parked the car so we could watch. The pilots all stood around smoking and letting their scarves blow in the wind. They looked other-worldly to me as I watched them with the curiosity of a 9-year old boy. Andy and I jumped out of the car and mustered the courage to approach their inner circle. With my best impersonation of Dick Tracy, I asked, "Excuse me sir, can we go up for a ride?"

The pilot turned around and looked at me, and with a chuckle answered, "Well I'd love to take you boys up, but we are getting ready to do a stunt show. Come back after the show and we'll see what we can do."

A stunt show, I looked at my cousin in disbelief. We had hit the jackpot. I had lucked out beyond belief as I had saved three dollars. The stunt show cost two dollars and the plane rides cost one dollar.

Andy asked, "Why do we have to pay to see the stunt show when we can just look up in the sky and see it?"

I told him, "Because you are paying those pilots to risk their lives. You can't expect them to do the show for free. Besides they have to pay for the fuel. How else can these guys make money?"

After the stunt show ended, we waited in a long line for our turn just like all the other kids. It seemed like we would never get to have our ride, I didn't care. I was prepared to wait as long as necessary for that exuberant soaring feeling again. Time goes by so slowly when you are young and it had been such a long time since I had my first ride. All the kids watched intently as each plane took off for the sky and then quickly landed. They were mesmerized and some were a little scared too.

The Wright Brothers had made their first flight in 1903 and it was now 1939. The public was starting to accept the fact that airplanes were the wave of the future. They realized that flying machines were engaged in the war in Europe and like the automobile they were here to stay.

At last, our turn came; I walked up to the shiny black airplane and looked into the pilot's eyes for a moment. He smiled and looked right back at me. He had a thin moustache and a black leather jacket with a yellow scarf. He asked, "You boys ever been up before?"

"Yes" I shouted out loud so he could hear me over the roar of the engine, "at the baseball field once".

Andy, my cousin looked scared, it was his first time.

"Well, hold onto your hats," he told us, then he lifted me in first, and my cousin sat beside me. It was a two-seater and we sat right behind the pilot. He steered the airplane out through the grass and began to go faster and faster. Suddenly we were airborne. That same euphoric feeling came over me again.

All the people on the ground became tiny; we could see all the rides on the fairgrounds. Seeing all these things above the World's Fair was amazing. I knew I wanted to be able to see the rest of the world from up here. Just as soon as we had taken off it was time to land. I shook hands with the pilot and thanked him. We paid him our dollar and continued on to the fair.

There were two very impressive things we saw that day at the World's Fair of 1939, the Perisphere and the Trylon. They were really the recognizable symbols of the fair. The Trylon, a three-sided pylon, stood 610 feet high and its companion, the Perisphere, measured 185 feet in diameter. Inside the Perisphere was the 'Democracy' exhibit and model of 'The City of the Future' built to house one million people. But what I remembered most was my airplane ride.

It was almost 1940 and we were hearing terrible things about the war in Europe. Mom and Dad didn't quite know what to say to us when we asked them questions about the war. They were still struggling to make ends meet and my oldest brother, Albert, was asked to get a job to help bring in money for the family. He was not fourteen yet, but got a job delivering milk. Although he didn't have a driver's license, he was responsible and looked older because he was tall. It didn't hurt either that he was polite. In high school, he was quite the scholar too. His specialties were science and mathematics. The folks were hoping he would be able to get a scholarship to pay for college. They instilled in us from an early age to work hard, get an education, make something of yourself and the fun will come later.

December 7, 1941 was a terrible day, and I still remember when we heard it on the radio. Albert had just turned fifteen, Freddie was thirteen and I was eleven. War rationing started very soon and Dad's business was affected, as certain items were unavailable in the grocery store. People needed books of rationing stamps for sugar. There were lots of items that people gave up for the military men. Thousands of men had to be fed, and Dad told us everybody had to make sacrifices in times like these, he didn't seem to mind. Mom used her word 'charity' a lot. And we all listened to the radio to find out what was happening to our boys overseas. People became very patriotic but no one really knew quite what to do and so we waited.

In just three short years, we were fully involved in World War II. The three of us boys speculated about the war; in just six months Albert would graduate from high school. I already knew what he was going to do, he had confided in Freddie and me. He hadn't told Mom and Dad yet. He was going to join the Navy as an enlisted man. We promised not to tell the folks, but one night two weeks before graduation, Freddie blurted it out at the dinner table.

Dad angrily yelled, "Absolutely not, you are going to go to college and get an education. You are not going to join the Navy. I don't want any of my boys getting killed over there!"

Dad knew he was not being patriotic and that what he had just said could not leave the house. If the community ever knew how he felt, they would not go into his store again. So, not one of us ever said a word about it again. Freddie and Albert, (who hadn't turned 18 yet) didn't speak to each other for two weeks.

Albert's high school graduation came and went. He had saved his money from his days as a milk delivery boy and his paper route. He got the scholarship he wanted to the college for a degree in chemistry. He still dreamed about flying but he loved ships too. Freddie took over his job as the milk delivery boy as he was now fifteen. I kept the paper route and saved every penny for college, because with one Thomas boy at college the others would soon follow.

Mom was still saving for that house on 59 Valley Street. Would there ever be a time when we didn't have to save every penny that came in? Freddie turned sixteen that summer and was in love with a local girl. They were always together and with Albert getting ready to go away to college, I was alone most of the time. At the ripe old age of fourteen, I would be starting high school and looking forward to studies that I hoped would propel me closer to airplanes. Dad still didn't know of my dreams; but Mom did, she understood me because she had dreams of her own.

The house at 59 Valley Street had just gone up for sale. The owners were asking $3500.00 and it was close to what Mom and Dad had saved. She would have to convince Dad, but she was good at that, so in the end Mom got her house. We moved into that house in the summer of 1944. Mom got her house so Dad was content at least for a while.

This new house had a small room off the stairs which became my airplane room, I must have spent half my life in there, building new model planes that had little gas engines. Aunt Ruth, mom's sister had given us boys these great models to build and fly and we could hardly wait to get them into the air. (And after I had a son of my own, I brought one of those old hand made planes from my New York homestead to California; and taught my son, Rich, to fly it. I wanted him to start flying and later he did solo at age 16.)

Well, Dad was almost happy, his oldest son was away at college, his middle son was working hard delivering milk and making good grades and his youngest son was getting ready to start high school. We three still were made to work on holidays! Whether we had to deliver ice or help out some other way, work always came first.

Dad was no slouch either, he wouldn't be accused of being non-patriotic, but he also didn't want his boys going to war and he didn't care what anyone thought. His world seemed to be falling into place until he received a letter from Albert that November. Albert had decided to leave college and join the Navy since he had just turned 18 and didn't need Dad's permission anymore. He told Dad, he would qualify for the GI Bill and return to college when he came back. Dad was really upset but he never said a word. He knew there was nothing he could do. Albert's mind was made up, so he enlisted in the Navy after all. When he came home at Christmas, he was in uniform and talked about the war in great detail. I listened to every word he said.

The stories he told me about the war were hard to believe. He explained that the German's had invented these new kinds of planes called 'jets'. These planes were able to go higher and faster than any of our own American planes, because they had a turbine engine that employed combustion. And if the Americans didn't do something pretty soon the other side might win the war.

These stories continued to excite me as he said the facts were that we had all kinds of spies working on codes to break the Germans secret plans. There were so many things to learn from his stories I didn't even think about reading my Dick Tracy books. Albert told me straight off, "Look you want to be like Dick Tracy, that's kid stuff. These men involved in the war effort are for real. They are the real heroes and don't you ever forget it."

Right then I decided to forget about 'kid's stuff' and concentrate on what was going on in the war. I decided to sign up for ROTC at school. At first Dad didn't like it but when he found out it would help give me money for college he gave his approval.

During this time Mom's brother, Uncle Almon came to visit with Albert. At dinner he let the cat out of the bag and asked, "Well Richie, do you still want to drive those flying machines?"

Dad looked at me in bewilderment, I answered, "Yes, I do", and looked right back at Dad as he rolled his eyes.

He was beginning to get used to the idea of his boys making their own decisions; could it be he was starting to soften a little bit? Freddie and I had worked on Uncle Almon's farm all summer. We confided in him about wanting to fly, and about building and flying the models. Dad was aware of our love for airplane models and the time spent building and flying them, he had to have some knowledge of our love for flying. I think in his heart he was just scared for us. But Mom's love for adventure and daring was in my blood.

In April, 1945, I turned fifteen and could now share the milk delivery job with Freddie; he was handling most all the ice deliveries by himself. He had chosen to study Geological Engineering and wanted to get rich finding oil. Making money was very important to him; Dad had really instilled the "get rich" syndrome in him.

Just when Albert had gone through training and was getting ready to ship out, the war ended. Dad was relieved. Albert was coming home; he would get all the benefits of the GI Bill and go back to college. Dad let us have a small gathering at the house. Albert returned to 59 Valley Street to a homecoming that would have made you think he was a war hero.

CHAPTER 4

MAYVILLE CENTRAL HIGH SCHOOL

✦

My first year in high school was uneventful. Mom made sure I took all the necessary courses so I could get into a good college. I studied hard and did well, because Dad expected me to get a scholarship just like both of my brothers.

I had two good friends, Rod Ross and Ed Seaton. Rod was an all around good guy, popular and the class president. He was a born leader and I wanted to be like him, so I ran for vice president and made it. I tagged along with him and we became close buddies. I was a shy person because of wearing glasses due to having had rheumatic fever. The doctor said I would grow out of it; but I still hadn't.

Determined to be a success, I followed Rod's lead and tried out for all three sports teams. Surprise, Dad's slave driving must have paid off for me, because I made the baseball team, the football team and the basketball team. I lettered every year in all three sports when I was in high school. This seemed to make Dad proud of me and I hoped I could win him over.

Still delivering papers and milk, I was studying hard and trying to find a better job. Finally I got a job setting pins at the bowling alley; it paid well and there were tips. When summer came I caddied at the Chautauqua Country Club Golf Course, where the big boys played golf. I had also learned how to play golf and was getting jobs caddying for the local duffers. But the big name golfers paid better and it would all come in handy to make my dreams of flying come true.

Dad was a sports fanatic and if I could prove to him that I was good in sports, it would be easier to get his support in what I wanted to do with my life. Hopefully he would support me in what I really wanted to be and that was a test pilot.

Graduation was an exciting time, the Class of 1948 had high hopes and I was looking forward to a new experience in my life. I had saved some money but I knew it would not be enough. I knew there would have to be hours and hours of work all summer.

Everyone stood around at the graduation party and talked about what they wanted to do. Meekly, I wanted to say, 'I want to be a test pilot,' but I felt I couldn't even say that to the kids, they wouldn't believe me anyway. So, I amended my comment to, "Well, I have plans to go to St. Louis University and major in Aeronautical Engineering."

"Nobody from Mayville has ever done anything like that," said one of the girls. "I'll believe that when I read it in the newspapers."

Later on I would make the local paper as Mayville's First Jet Pilot. It would come as a surprise to me and everyone else as well. But for now, I knew my dreams were a long shot. All the kids went back to enjoying themselves and my comment was forgotten.

That summer there was back breaking hard work at Uncle Almon's farm, along with odd jobs. I saved every cent I made toward achieving my goal. I ran into a lot of the old gang, but I couldn't fritter away time doing those fun things I wanted. My plans were set to go to Parks College in the fall and I knew sticking to my plan now would help with the hard studying ahead of me. It would be a serious mistake to screw this up.

There was one thing I knew; I wanted to be a pilot, not just any pilot but a test pilot. It was a combination of all the things we had talked about as kids, the adventure, the knowledge, the excitement and the glory. After all, I realized test piloting was not something one does haphazardly. As a precise science, it involved skill, courage and most of all knowledge. Heavy-duty engineering courses awaited me at Parks Aeronautical College of St. Louis University. I hoped with all my heart I would be ready.

CHAPTER 5

PARKS AERONAUTICAL COLLEGE OF ST LOUIS UNIVERSITY

✦

By the fall of 1948, I had saved $1500.00 for Parks Aeronautical College. When I arrived and met the Dean of Education, he explained in detail why I should not go into engineering. Then he kept questioning me as to why I wanted to get an aeronautical engineering degree. I tried to explain to him all the reasons that had led to my decision.

The Dean's answer to me was "Look engineers are walking the street right now and they can't get jobs, wouldn't you rather do something else?"

A definite "No" was my answer "that is what I came to this college to study and that is what I want to do."

When he finally realized that he couldn't sway my decision, he left me alone and I was free to pursue my goal. Flying was something I had to do. It was serious business and my utmost desire all my life; of course, this was just the beginning and I still had a long way to go.

During my college years I was able to get a job on weekends polishing and cleaning airplanes at Frontier Airlines. McDonnell Douglas hired college students for drafting jobs because they could get us cheaper. We drew things like brackets, parts and other odds and ends. I guess they weren't impressed with my drawing because they never offered me a position.

Along with working part-time on weekends I had a heavy load of courses to keep up. This is where having a college roommate somewhat older came in handy. Tom Gillespie was about six years older and already a pilot. He was attending Parks College on the GI Bill. He knew the ropes and showed me how to study. Without his help I might not have made it. Along with being a pilot, Tom was also a coach and taught me how to relax with a tough schedule of studying. To break the monotony, we would spend a few hours each week shooting hoops and having a little fun.

But more importantly, Tom spent many hours telling me about flying, giving me inside information only an experienced veteran can offer. Here I was just a young kid out of high school and I really admired him. He definitely made an impact on the course I took in life. His experience as a pilot sounded so daringly exciting. But, he emphasized the hard work involved. His honest revelation into flying gave me a dosage of reality of what to expect if I really wanted to be a test pilot.

Parks College was demanding and soon the first year was over, most of my money was gone. My folks were afraid that I'd get there and run out of money. Then how would we pay for it. My future was written clearly on the wall. In order for me to finish college I would have to finance it by myself, with a little bit of help from them. It was going to be rough, but I intended to finish my degree. Determined to finish out my three years and graduate, I wasn't going to let lack of funds stop me. So, summer came and I went home and worked all the old jobs. The folks didn't see how I was going to be able to make a living as a pilot, but I kept convincing them I could.

As soon as I got back to college I got a job setting pins at night until the bowling alley closed. There were several courses to take before I was able to learn how to fly the Stearman biplane. I knew it was coming soon and I was getting really excited and mentally prepared for what was awaiting me. Setting pins at night is a tough job and physically exhausting. Then trying to study after that until 2 a.m. or later on an empty stomach is a real challenge too.

I think if you told college students that they could learn to fly aircraft as part of their college courses, universities would generate a lot more interest in potential students than they do now. Of course it is the ultimate extra curricular activity and you have to keep your grades up like anything else. I will tell you, further on down the road the subject of grades came back to haunt me when I applied for the astronaut candidate program. NASA turned me down because I had three D's in my major. So you see, employers can exclude for reasons like that and they don't have to justify it because every cat and dog that could fly at that time applied to be an astronaut. Naturally, only the very exceptional few were chosen.

After completing my courses in math and engineering I was ready to take my turn in the Stearman biplane. My dream was beginning to unfold, I was learning to fly. It wasn't test flying because most do something wrong when you are just starting and it was no different in my case. Those Stearman planes had been around for fifty years, but once I had flown one, I was kind of stamped as a 'test pilot'. Strange as it may seem, in those days, suddenly people labeled you a test pilot. But with the degree in aeronautical engineering, a little experience and the right connections, somebody might actually hire you. At least that was what I imagined at the time. I started out in the biplane and when I graduated college in 1952, I felt like I was ready for anything; however, I was not!

CHAPTER 6

465TH FIGHTER INTERCEPTR SQUADRON

✦

In March of 1952, at the great age of 22 years, I was commissioned as 2nd Lieutenant in the Air Force through the ROTC program. Now I was really on my way. Convincing my folks that I could make a living now that I had the commission and had completed college would be an easy quest. It was true; I could earn some kind of living flying jets. In fact, I'll never forget that first check that I received, I felt like I was rich as it was $600. This money was to buy dress uniforms and the necessary paraphernalia to go with them. I'll never forget the first time I put that uniform on and looked at myself in the mirror. The image emboldened me to become the person I wanted to be.

MY FIRST OFFICIAL AIR FORCE PICTURE

My first assignment was in May of 1952, which was for primary training at Marana Air Force Base, Arizona. Some of us got to fly the T-6 and I soloed in it as well, then on to basic training. Our basic training was about six weeks which included complete instrument checkout. We were actually capable of demonstrating landings on the runway without seeing the ground. Day after day for that six-week period we practiced those take-offs and landings to become proficient in making instrument landings. We didn't have the equipment they have now that would almost land the plane for you. The instructors must have had a lot of nerve to watch us as we weren't very accurate to begin with. We were actually flying blind you might say. A hood was put over the canopy so you could not see out at all! You had to rely on your instruments to tell you when to touch down and there were some frightening moments when you weren't very sure of yourself. It was a fantastic step forward when I earned those wings. As those beautiful silver wings were pinned on my uniform, there was a hint of distinction in my heartfelt feelings, a reward for the work I had done to earn them. It must feel that way to every pilot who earns those emblems of dedication.

There were about 250 new pilots training in this squadron. The buzz was on and being a pilot was the thing a lot of guys wanted to do. A few new friends were made, but time constraints were such that we didn't have a lot of time for socializing, still we did find time to relax. One of my new friends was a great guy named Glen Wallin. We sort of organized our own small group that would get together when we had time, and needed a little R&R.

Along with having a good time every now and then, Glen and I became great friends. We rode Harleys together in Arizona and we exchanged stories of our years growing up. Both of us were influenced to fly because of the dashing uniform and those perilous adventures of WWII. The two of us were almost the same age, except Glen was married and had three little children. Our squadron was transferred out to San Marcos, Texas for advance training, Phase I. It was January 1953.

Glen's wife Tina was always trying to fix me up since I was single. Every once in a while they would find me a blind date, but no one ever caught my fancy. Glen and I were flying jets and living our dreams playing 'tick, tack, toe' in the sky and pretending to be war aces. Although, my main focus was to concentrate on flying.

As Phase I ended, we were transferred to James Connolly AFB in Waco, Texas, for jet training in the T-33's and eventually graduation in Class 53D. After four months, Glen and I both made the cut; we were flying those T-33's and loving it. We had completed sixty or seventy hours of time in the T-33's, and had approximately 300 hours of flight time under our belts. By now all of us were extremely proficient in instrument flying and were each assigned to an airplane.

Then for our next assignment, we were sent to Tyndall AFB in Panama City, Florida, for all weather flights in the F-86D Fighters. We thought it couldn't get any better…Florida… summer time… the beach, and flying F-86D Fighters. Still riding our Harleys, we had the greatest world just flying jets and riding Harleys on the beach. We really tore it up on our motorcycles. We hung out at the beach in Panama City and flew jets the rest of the time, it was an idyllic life-style and I seemed to have no cares in the world.

During that summer there was a guy named Gibb Kilder in our outfit and he was just something of a daredevil when it came to flying. One night just horsing around, Gibb flew his T-33 about 50 feet off the deck through the drive-in movies. He flew right in front of the screen at about 200 knots. The shock wave afterwards left cars honking and people screaming, for an instant anyway, until they realized what had taken place. He sure got their attention. It didn't go so good for me though as I got called in and blamed for it! I swear I never did it; but nobody would believe me and I never did squeal to anyone that it was ol' Kilder.

Glen and I continued to rip it up on the beach at night with our Harleys. We rode as fast as we could through the sand right up to the water. It was crazy and I can't imagine why we didn't break our necks, but that was the only thing I was guilty of doing. Those wild rides weren't meant to last though; and October of '53, I was assigned to the 465th Fighter Interceptor Squadron at McCord AFB in Washington State. Later that squadron became the 318th FIS.

In 1954 on a cross country mission in the T-33, two of us flew over the Grand Canyon. We both had agreed to fly one mile down into the canyon going 300-400 knots/hr, sashaying in and out of the canyon walls 2 or 3,000 feet higher. We followed the river up to Williams, Arizona. This wasn't anything new, lots of pilots were guilty of doing this trick and some were still there because they had hit a wall and crashed. At the time we did it, there were no rules broken, but later accidents put a stop to the practice because someone made a mistake and crashed into a wall or hit a cable which ran 580 feet above the river.

A Naval aviator buzzing the canyon scared a motorist on the road and caused an accident. The authorities investigated the aircraft from the Navy for two years and checked witnesses with everybody in the area. It was speculated that the airplane came from the 29 Palms Naval Air Station. Fortunately for the pilot, he was never caught. They had all pilots from the squadron swear to their statements, but if they knew they never told.

I was always getting 'picked on' by these two majors accusing me of buzzing someone, even though I was not guilty. I had buzzed a guy one time in an open field going about 600 miles/hr. I went over his field, pulled up, looked at the city and went back to base. I never told anyone because I knew it could really damage my flying career.

Mt. Rainier, which was shaped by the volcanic cone, was eroded at the very top. Photographers were always interested in taking pictures of the top and several of us agreed to fly through the U-shape in formation. There was a ski resort near the top so we had to be very careful and stay away from that because of the ski lifts. One could get tangled up in that and cause a disaster. But, a lot of us would fly over the hole at the top; I took a lot of neat pictures. With two or three planes in formation flying over the top, the pictures were fantastic. Pilots would think 'gee whiz' look at that!

My Commanding Officer authorized me to take a picture for an elderly gentleman in Tacoma, Washington. This old guy's dog was buried out in a field near a little town next to Tacoma. He had written a letter to the base commander and requested a salute to his dog! So believe it or not, three of us in F-86's did an actual fly-over. We came in very low and went across the dog's grave, and I took the picture of the grave for the old man. We received a letter from him afterwards thanking us for the formal formation fly over. Actually, you feel pretty good giving some old guy a salute for his dog. It was an act of public relations to sooth the community for all the pilots breaking the sound barrier. Strange the things that stick with you as the years pass.

While skiing on Mt. Rainier, I remembered that vertigo can result in an accident. I had a severe case of vertigo in the F-86D, during an Air Defense Command mission. We were pulling high G's on instruments and I made an error on instruments, my let down was below minimum altitude to make a safe recovery, this caused excessive G's (three G's) which induced vertigo. I had to grab the stick with both hands, ignore the instrument panel and force myself to hold one position until I was fully recovered from the vertigo condition. This was during the 465th Aero Squadron training at McCord AFB, Washington State.

The last time I remember getting the condition was in the 1969 air races from Milwaukee to Reno. This was probably caused by watching the propeller speed rotation being calibrated to sync too long, while standing on the ground. After starting to taxi I actually lost control of the Corsair airplane due to vertigo. I taxied back in, it was so bad. Sometimes it was so strenuous you felt like you could fall right out of the cockpit onto the ground. So you need the discipline of science for the necessities of life! Of course, I got over it and took off after a few minutes.

During my time at McCord AFB, I had a rare experience that I would always wonder about in later life. Late one night about 10 o'clock my squadron was scrambled on a report of a UFO over the Pacific Ocean, approximately three miles southeast of Seattle, at 1500 ft off the ocean deck. There was no moon that night, the ocean looked like the black hole of Hades or the cave of despair; and as we took off I had an eerie feeling. This was a very dangerous mission and I didn't like it. You get this creepy feeling all over on a flight like this, you're trying to stay focused on the low altitude and proximity of the ocean. And, spooked about what or who you might encounter, and then what do you do if you see something strange?

We three pilots were in constant radio contact with each other. After searching the skies in the area we had been ordered to fly, no unusual object or light was found. As squadron leader I gave the order to return to base. Let me say that flying over the ocean on a obscure black night at only 1500 feet, searching for a UFO, was about the most terrifying experience I had had up to this point. Little did I know that I and my aircraft would subsequently become an unidentifiable flying object (UFO) later in life.

Not too long after this assignment Glen was flying the T-33 again. We both found ourselves back in that plane. Unfortunately Glen was involved in a malfunction, a flame-out occurred. The cockpit went black and the whole instrument panel went out. The airplane literally fell out of the sky to the runway and he was killed instantly, leaving behind Tina and their three children. When Glen was killed, I was really torn up about it for a long time after. Sometimes people who knew Glen would ask me about him. I thought he was one of the nicest guys I had ever met, and the questions would go deeper. Things most people don't like to think about, the inevitable, death. Did Glen go to heaven? If a place like that exists, I'm sure he did.

I'm not a person who likes to discuss private beliefs and political opinions. But I can tell you I would have my turn with the wicked T-33 as well. Fortunately I would turn out to be one of the lucky ones, a survivor.

My time in the Air Force was winding down and I was undecided. Should I stay for more or leave for the unknown? Well it seems my life was always pushing for the unknown. So I gave the Air Force my resignation instead of my re-up and said my goodbyes to my friends.

CHAPTER 7

WICHITA, KANSAS – 1956

✦

I was fresh out of the Air Force and needing a job. I knew the only kind of job I wanted was a flying job. My next move was seeking out a few of my college friends. The Air Force career had been great and I had certainly made lots of friends there, but those guys were staying. I knew if I really wanted to fly 'new' stuff, I had to get a job with the manufacturers.

During college, I had to keep my nose to the grindstone to make it through; but I did find time to join a fraternity. This association came in handy later on after the Air Force career was over. I contacted several of my fraternity brothers who were in the aerospace industry for help in finding employment. My close friend and ex-roommate, Tom Guillespie, was in Flight Test management at Beech Aircraft. He didn't hesitate putting in a good word for me and I was hired by Beech in 1956 as a Flight Test Engineer. In a few weeks I moved to Production Flight Test as a production pilot, but mostly on Bonanzas. It wasn't all that exciting.

My forte was jets, and flying Beechcrafts was just a holding pattern, or a stepping stone to bigger and better aircraft. So in September, 1956, I joined the Kansas Air National Guard to fly F-80C's. Keeping current in jets was very important to me and I knew that to do anything in the world of experimental flying, it would have to be with jet powered aircraft.

Beech Aircraft proved to be a rather interesting place though in lots of ways. I would be privileged to put hours on a new model they had just designed and built. It was the Travel Air, an upscale twin engine private plane; something that would attract the rich and famous. The trouble was they didn't really have enough work for me. So I was relegated to do the mail run to Harrington, Kansas, where Beech had a small sub-contractor plant. This trip was flown in the single engine Bonanza, an ornery little V-tailed bird that could get you in trouble in severe weather.

Harrington, Kansas, was a farming community and boring most of the time, unless you got creative with the airplane. During those frequent trips I would trim the airplane in such a way I could crawl into the back seat and fly it. If you leaned to the front, the airplane would nose down slightly and to reverse that mode, you leaned to the back and the nose would come up. The same principal was applied to the turns, if you leaned to the left, the plane would bank slightly left and vice versa.

There were other little experiments I discovered to be interesting too. I found I could land the plane in a much shorter distance than usually required. However that trick didn't turn out so good, as I tried that little stunt one morning after a rather good rain storm the night before. The runway in Harrington was wet and the plane skidded off the end into a nasty field of mud. I found that when your wheels are mired to the hub no amount of power is going to move you. Consequently, I had to hire a farmer nearby to bring his John Deere tractor and pull the Bonanza out of the mud, much to my chagrin. Those fellow pilots back at the plant in Wichita heard about this and were relentless in their convivial pestering of me over this Thomas escapade. But, not to worry, I would surely give them more fuel for their fire.

The month I hired into Beech Aircraft, they were preparing for their annual International Distributor's Convention, which they held there at the plant. The new Bonanza cabin mock-ups were displayed actual size, color and instrumentation exactly as they would be in the airplane. They had a live model demonstrating the new features to the crowd of distributors as the sales representative explained in detail the feature or cockpit revision that had been made. My friend Tom, advised me to go to the meeting to get acquainted with the new aspects of the Bonanza.

There didn't seem to be any place for me to sit as I was a new hire and the organizers had not remembered to put me on the pilot list (actually I wasn't a pilot yet, that's why). So I stood quietly at the back of this large room and took it all in. During this time a cute little gal I had seen working on 'Mahogany Row' was the live model in the cockpit and doing the demonstrating of the new products.

I had noticed her on several occasions walking through the huge engineering drafting room where I was assigned at the time. Whenever she paraded down the isle carrying papers to the Chief Engineer's office, I wasn't the only flight test engineer who watched. That room was filled with at least sixty or seventy guys. There were drafting tables and desks interspersed over most of the room. Then a long isle separated the east side where cubicles of half polished wood and half glass made private offices for the different project engineers and the chief engineer. Their respective secretaries sat at desks in front of those offices.

It was one of those times that I happened to be in the Chief Engineer's office that she delivered papers from Contract Administration up to his office. As she stood there talking to his secretary, she glanced through the window and I was intently watching her. She looked straight at me and I thought she smiled at me; but maybe it was the fact she was talking to the secretary and something funny had been said. Then she left and I assumed she went to her own working area. When I left the Chief's office, I quietly asked his secretary her name and if she had her telephone number. The secretary quickly told me her name was Cynda and she worked for James Lew, the Vice President of Contract Administration on Mahogany Row. Well, I decided to take a stroll down to Mahogany Row, she didn't actually work for Mr. Lew, but she worked as a secretary for one of his contract administrators. I was able to get her phone number at work and called her for a blind date. That was the start of a long term relationship…I guess you'd call it.

Wichita would prove to be a life changing experience. The Kansas plains were not all that interesting, but the local scenery seemed to keep my interest. Although Beech's airplanes were very classy private craft, the testing was not what I wanted. There were some perks that I found more interesting. As I mentioned, the newest plane on the line was a Twin Beech called the Travel Air, which later became the Beech Baron. Because it hadn't been certified by the FAA yet, the factory needed flying time put on this very expensive aircraft. Luckily, I was one of those pilots who got to fly it cross country to log the hours.

Now Cynda thought I was a pretty big deal since I could take her on a flying date. I thought I was a pretty big deal myself. Later on after one of those week ends when I flew her to Oklahoma to see her brother Phillip and his family, she felt the brunt of her week end date. She was teased by some of the guys at work the following Monday about joining the 'mile high group'. She didn't know what they meant, but after I explained it to her, she stood up for herself without a hint of humor. No need to worry about this one taking any heat! She could dish it out too.

During these next few months of courting this little gal, I was trying hard to make my mark in the Kansas Air National Guard by getting as much flying time in as possible. She was not one to stay put at home. But, I was having the time of my life going on cross country trips with a couple of single KANG pilots. We would fly into Austin, Texas, on Friday night and stay through Saturday night and come home Sunday. Mike and Pat Windsor were twins that flew with the Guard and we became flying buddies. We liked Austin, Texas, so much we decided to invest in a small pizza business near the college campus. This gave me even more excuses to be gone on the week ends.

Cynda's roommates were giving her advice about this new guy… me… and it wasn't good. She wasn't going to sit around and wait for me to ask her for a date. It happened that Major Bob von Romberg and his wife, Joy, lived in the other side of the duplex that I and another single guy shared. Cynda and I had become somewhat acquainted with them. Joy worked in the next department over from Cynda at Beech. The two of them quickly put their heads together and plotted against me. There weren't a lot of places to go in Wichita, most were dives in those days and the Officer's Club at McConnell AFB really was the nicest place to hang out.

It was one of those weekends I was counting on a cross country flight, when I found out at the last minute the plane was down for maintenance. Those gals had cooked up a double-cross for me and I fell right into their net. It seems Joy had suggested that Cynda get herself a good dancing date and join them at the Officer's Club on Friday night. It wasn't very hard for Cynda to find herself a date and so, she did that. Joy and Bob were friends of mine, I thought, well Bob was anyway. So after calling Cynda late for the Friday night dance at the club and getting turned down, I decided to go to the club alone. It was a regular place for the officers to hang out alone anyway. Little did I know the lair had been set?

When I arrived at the club, I got an unpleasant surprise. There sitting in the booth with Joy and Bob was my girl with some other guy. I was jealous and I guess just plain mad. I proceeded to get myself pretty intoxicated, as I sat at the bar and watched Cynda performing on the dance floor with her date. I decided he could dance almost as well as I could, maybe even better and that added fuel to the fire. I was bursting with indignation until I felt I would explode after watching them dance for a couple of hours. Finally, when I just couldn't stand it any longer, I got up from the bar stool and walked to the booth where they were sitting and laughing.

Then I leaned over the table to Cynda and said, "You think you are so damn smart!" With that said, it was time for me to make my exit from the club.

I drove my baby blue Cadillac convertible to a close location near Cynda's duplex and parked. I was waiting for her to come home so I could talk to her. It wasn't long before her date pulled up in front, walked her to the door, kissed her goodnight and left. She went inside and I was so mad that he kissed her; I decided to just go on to my place. When I got home, I had changed my mind again; instead I gave in and called her for a date for the next night.

The phone rang and rang, but the minute she answered the phone, still slightly inebriated I blurted out, "OK, you win we are going steady. Do we have a date for tomorrow night?"

Can you believe it, she was giggling and sweetly said, "OK to the first and yes to the second question. I'll see you at 7." Then she hung up.

I don't know who was more jealous of whom, 'cause she put up some pretty nasty fights on my behalf too. There was this gal at Beech, her last name was Honeycutt; well I don't have to go into much explanation to tell you what the guys said about Larena with a last name like that. She was a large girl, attractive and had her eye on me for some reason. She found my telephone number at home somehow and started calling me inviting me over to her place. I would tell Cynda about her calls and that caused Cynda to throw quite a howling fit. I never knew if Cynda actually told her where she could go, but the threats that came out were very entertaining. Cynda was about half the size of Larena, as she was about as tall as I was, so I doubt if Cynda ever did pick a fight with her!

CHAPTER 8

THE T-33 CRASH AND AMUSING TRIPS

✦

It was on one of those weekends when Pat Windsor and I had gone cross country in the T-33 to Austin, Texas, to check on our Pizza Mia restaurant. The weather had been very nasty during the weekend and we were getting ready to leave and fly back to McConnell Air Force Base. It was Sunday night as we took off in a blinding rain towards Wichita, Kansas. Most of the trip was uneventful except for the rain; but as we passed over Blackwell, Oklahoma, whatever happened would cause us extreme displeasure in the next few minutes.

When we did our walk-around check in Austin it was storming with lightning and thunder, the rain pelting down. You don't want to point the finger at anyone in particular, but the afterburner door may have been left open; and we were taking off in the rain storm. So maybe rain got into the engine and shorted the electrical system out. At any rate a malfunction occurred in the engine. I'm not certain of everything that went wrong. But when we pulled the throttle off, or came off idle on the throttle, it'd go to a thousand degrees; so naturally you weren't inclined to use that very much. At idle it was running fairly well, and we decided we'd put it into McConnell Air Force Base where we were headed anyway. Because of the electrical failure, we couldn't jettison our full tip tanks. And, we couldn't punch out earlier as there was no electrical power to blow the canopy off. Therefore, we couldn't bail out.

Unfortunately it didn't work out as well as it could have because we had to land downwind. We didn't have enough power to make the distance to land upwind. During the downwind landing, we were a little slow and too low, so that when we came in we stalled. The plane dropped like a rock hitting crooked with the wing tip down; and the tip tank struck the runway. That was probably good because when the tank hit the concrete, that threw us over sideways which sheared the gear, and the sheared main gear let us down easy instead of rolling us up in a ball.

Then the nose gear came whacking down on the ground and that started the plane spinning. So we went spinning down the infield of the McConnell runway. Well, that was bad in one way but it was good in another. It tore the bottom of the airplane all open and let all the fuel out. At the time, we didn't know that, but had the fuel been in the tank behind the cockpit, well we would have been fried. Anyway with fuel coming out, I don't know whether it was the rocks or hot engine or whatever, something ignited this fuel. All of a sudden we had this blaze, this great fire going up the middle of the runway as we're spinning around and counting the number of times that we saw the Boeing hanger go by. Why you do that I have no idea but it was something we did.

The electrical system had totally malfunctioned and we were completely helpless. We slid to a stop and then the fire caught up with us. We're sitting in the middle of a blazing bunch of airplane. It's strange, there's a little crank in there so you can manually crank the canopy open. It is a useless piece of material because it takes, I don't know, hundreds of rotations to get the canopy up. I frantically pushed up on the canopy from inside because I was in the back seat and I was promptly burned…I didn't have my helmet on. T-33's were very tight for tall guys and since I was pushing six feet, I couldn't wear my helmet comfortably in the rear seat. The T-33 has a tandem cockpit and for me to get out, Pat had to manually crank the canopy up much higher which let the flames shoot in around his helmet and face. To make matters even worse I had my parachute pack on also. The canopy was already so hot that it burned the top of my head. Thank God, we had miraculously slid to a stop.

The McConnell firefighters saved our lives as they were there immediately with their foam and put the fire out. The base hospital's emergency team actually pulled us out of the airplane. Together, they got us out of the aircraft and put us in their ambulances to go to the base facility. Lucky for us, both the McConnell teams were superior in their rescue.

The pilot, Pat Windsor, in the front seat, had tried desperately to crank the canopy open enough to get me out. Consequently he had first, second and third degree burns on the sides of his face and his hands. There were huge blisters which healed without any scars but he looked awful for a few days. We both had serious smoke inhalation; and I had first and second degree burns on my hands and the top of my head. We had both inhaled so much smoke that the doctor diagnosed us with 'singed' lungs. The real miracle, of this horrific crash, was we both survived to fly again!

Realizing that we had just cheated death, and were under a doctor's care in the base hospital, our adrenalin had kicked in and we were joking about the crash. About then the Kansas Air National Guard General came to check on us. He didn't chastise us too severely, but advised us that if there were any more incidences we would probably be asked to resign! Later we were cleared and it was found to be a system malfunction. The investigation wasn't very harsh, we were questioned a lot and the base maintenance in Austin was investigated or put on alert, but nothing serious came of the crash. I was flying for Beech at the time too, and they were concerned about me but considered me very lucky to have survived.

I had a date that night with Cynda, she was not patiently waiting for me to call as I was at least an hour late at this point. Finally I could get to a phone in the hospital room; it was full of KANG personnel and officers, the Wichita press and the hospital medical team checking us out. Pat's family had just arrived too. When I did get through to Cynda, she started to get her dander up. When I explained that we had just crashed a T-33 and burned on the McConnell runway, she felt awful. News of the crash came on the Wichita TV station shortly after and she jumped in her little red Ford convertible and made a mad dash for the base hospital. I think that was the first time we realized we really needed each other. I was glad to see her and asked her to call my mother in New York and tell her I was going to be all right. They kept us overnight and released us the next day. The plane was totaled and left a huge black streak down the runway where the fire had burned. I think you could say this was the beginning of a string of rather neglectful incidences that would wake me up to taking care of business someday!

◆   ◆   ◆

THE NEW YORK TRIP

On Labor Day 1957, Beech needed to have a Bonanza delivered to White Plains, New York. It seemed like a golden opportunity to see my folks. The fall colors were extraordinary at that time of the year and Cynda had never been to New York or met my folks. It would be a great trip and Beech agreed to pay for our air fare back to Wichita. It was a little different than the normal trip but I think Cynda's explanation will be better than mine.

Cynda's story; "My first exciting episode began when Dick was to deliver the Bonanza to White Plains. The plan was to deliver me to Jamestown, drop me off with his parents from Mayville, at the end of Chautauqua Lake, then take the airplane on to White Plains. He would catch a commercial jet back to Jamestown; and we would pick him up there later that evening."

"All started out pretty good, until Dick noticed we were low on fuel because of a strong headwind, I think! Dick started looking at the map and luckily found a small airfield at Upper Sandusky, Ohio. He quickly put the Bonanza down on that tiny airstrip to refuel. There was a field of tall cornstalks on one side and a casket company on the other! And the hard dirt airstrip was only as wide as a one lane road. That was a real eye-opener. The rest of the way wasn't exactly smooth either, as he fought a bumpy headwind all the way. When we finally got to Jamestown, the runway was slanted slightly downhill. I'm not sure if he was supposed to land going uphill or what, anyway his landing was short and he finally got stopped close to the end of the runway. Chautauqua Lake was near the end of the runway!"

"We were about an hour later than expected. Dad and Mom Thomas were there to meet us, Dick quickly left me with two strangers, got back in the airplane and took off for White Plains. He was supposed to take a commercial flight back that evening from White Plains to Jamestown, but he missed that flight and had to wait till the next day to fly into Jamestown. So I spent the first evening with his parents alone. Dad Thomas was not the friendliest dad I had ever met, but Mom was a peach and I fell in love with her right away. When Dick arrived the next day, things improved a little, and the following day we flew commercial back to Wichita. Whew!"

"I've heard of guys making the excuse of 'running out of fuel' in cars while dating a girl, but 'running out of fuel'…in an airplane! Well that takes a real imagination."

◆   ◆   ◆

THE TRIP TO CARACAS

It wasn't long after that Beech Aircraft organized a sales trip to South America. Several pilots and the Contract Administration sales team flew our demonstrator Beechcrafts to Caracas, Venezuela. I was one of the lucky pilots to get to go. Being the adventure loving guy, this was right up my alley. We were to be there four to six weeks demonstrating the different airplanes we had flown down there. The Venezuelans were very friendly and hospitable. It was a party every night and lots of fine ladies. It was my (good?) fortune to be entertained on the first night by Miss Caracas of 1955. Might I add she singled me out? Wow, what a dancer. So the next few weeks she taught me how to do the rumba, the samba, the mambo and tried to teach me the tango. I always thought I was a good dancer but the tango didn't seem to work out for me, looking back that was probably a lucky thing.

We finished our sales job at about five weeks and had to leave. Miss Caracas didn't want me to leave, but there was someone waiting for me at home; should I ever tell her about Miss Caracas? Cynda was waiting for me with open arms when we got back to Beech in Wichita. We had talked about getting married before I left and had been going steady for quite a while. So on May 2, 1958 we were married in the First Christian Church, Wichita, Kansas.

It wasn't long after we were married that Cynda found out about Miss Caracas, she had written me a couple of letters and sent her picture in her bathing suit. I had stuffed her letters and some other incriminating evidence in a small zip canvas bag when we moved into our first apartment and Cynda was organizing the closet when she discovered the bag. I think we had been married about a month! It wasn't a nice homecoming that evening when I got there from work. I was caught with a rather wormy situation, I guess I should have destroyed those to begin with and why I didn't I'll never know.

CHAPTER 9

FROM BEECH TO BOEING

✦

In May of 1958, I left Beech and was hired by Boeing as a Flight Test Engineer. I was still flying with the Kansas Air National Guard and was promoted to Captain in October, 1958. At that time I was flying the F-86L or basic F-86D.

The following January 1959, Boeing made me an Experimental Test Pilot and Chase Pilot. So now, I started flying the B-47, B-52, F-86F, and the T-33 for Boeing. In June of that year Boeing obtained F-100D's for chase support and I flew to Los Angeles to check out in that plane at the North American-Edwards facility as the Boeing pilot. Bob Baker, North American's Chief Pilot did the checking out, and in later years our paths would cross again.

When I left Beech and went to fly for Boeing, it was to fly fighter chase airplanes that Boeing had. The Air Force wanted the airplanes to support their test programs, which were the B-52 and the B-47. I went over there not planning to really get involved in big airplanes, but the opportunity comes up and somebody shoves you in. So I started flying the B-47's and the B-52's. Quite a drastic change for a fighter guy! Most fighter pilots wouldn't like that, but things come along like that opportunity and you don't know whether it's a good knock or a bad knock. But Boeing had this B-47 program which nobody in flight test wanted to fly because the pilots all wanted to be on the new version of the B-52 presently being built, the B-52G.

So somebody said, "Well, let Thomas go and be the co-pilot on the B-47. We'll give him 50 hours and that'll qualify him to check out in the B-52."

And when I did that it ended up that instead of getting fifty hours, once they got me in the airplane they just left me there and I got about two hundred hours. I was well qualified by that time at two hundred hours of B-47 time. You started out in the right seat and you could turn the fuel selections and then they gradually expanded your capability, you could fly and you could change the balance of fuel. It seemed like you could go on and on like this forever. They took me through all that and I went from chasing the B-52 to being a radar target with F-86's, F-100's and F-101's. The B-52 was the Air Force's critical program so you could get almost any kind of airplane you wanted. In fact, we had three F-100's when active duty people weren't able to get 100's or F-101's. We would go to Tucson to the bone yard and pick out one and they'd bring it out and away we would go.

I was having the time of my life. I'd make sonic booms all over Kansas, I mean, just really tore the place up! The F-86 didn't have enough thrust to break the sound barrier in level flight or even in a shallow dive. So the technique was to take it up to 45,000 ft, roll inverted, and pull it into a vertical dive (split S maneuver). This was a hell of a rush, you'd go past MACH 1 at about 18,000 ft, (couldn't read the spinning altimeter), throttle back, pop the speed brakes and pull out of the dive around 10,000 ft altitude. You are just a few seconds before going into a smoking hole in the ground!

Finally we traded the F-86's in for F-100's and that airplane would go supersonic in level flight. All the pilots that broke the sound barrier got the North American MACH Busters pin. That was before the days when they used to have to record every supersonic flight that was made. There were sonic booms constantly back in the sixties, and it was so neat, we liked doing it. But somebody out there didn't like it and eventually, we couldn't even fly supersonic. If we did we got into trouble.

During this time, Boeing Airplane Company started a comprehensive experiment to determine the effects of low frequency vibrations on human performance. These tests were being conducted under an Office of Naval research contract. A group of volunteers was subjected to five levels of low frequency vibrations. Information gained would be used by Boeing human factor engineers to establish base lines for further experiments.

The program lasted about two years. Facts on relationship between vibration and efficient human performance were expected to be yielded by the tests. This information could be used by design engineers working on aircraft and space ships of the future.

Volunteers taking part in the studies would be instrumented so necessary medical data could be obtained. Vibration levels were measured in the initial phase of the study and were defined as barely perceptible, definitely perceptible, annoying, maximum under which any man could work for a long period of time and maximum for brief, efficient performance.

The volunteer could push a button whenever he thought he had reached any of the five levels during the test. His verbal opinion would be recorded throughout each test. As you may have guessed by now, I was one of the volunteers who participated in these tests. At the time I didn't think they were dangerous, but as I look back on them now, they may have had something to do with my Parkinson's disease. Those hours and hours of vibrating gyrations probably didn't do me any good anyway.

VIBRATION TEST SEAT IN ACTION, DICK THOMAS

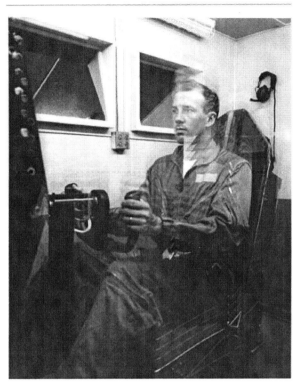

Then Boeing assigned me to fly a program on ERB-47E, I'm not able to tell you what the program was at the time, but we used to fly into Wright Patterson AFB and to this day when I visit the base I can't tell you where they parked us. It was a top secret classified program and they parked us far out in the field and put armed guards with loaded guns patrolling the perimeter. So I flew that for a while and then began to fly B-52's.

When I started flying the B-52's I was sent to Wright-Patterson for a special high altitude pressure flying suit and helmet. After getting that outer space-looking wear I was assigned to fly on a program of the max altitude of 55,000 feet. This was a flight test project to develop the proper maneuver for maximum separation from simulated atomic bomb drops. Dale Felix was pilot at the time and I was co-pilot.

PICTURE OF CREW WITH HIGH ALTITUDE PRESSURE SUIT

Real men from Mars!! In this picture from the left to right, are Glenn Botsford, experimental test pilot; Henry Walters, navigator; Richard Thomas, experimental test pilot; Thomas Bowman, equipment technician; Eugene Chase, navigator; and Russ Hunt, crew training and equipment supervisor. This crew engaged in test missions over 50,000 feet utilizing MC-3 pressure suits shown here. The suits provided pressurization for the arms and legs through capstans running the length of each extremity while a fully pressurized bladder provided protection for the torso.

Dale Felix and I flew those very high altitude tests in the B-52 at Edwards AFB on 3 March 1960. Dale thinks it was the highest altitude the B-52 had been flown to date. It was probably the B-52's highest and lowest altitudes that had ever been flown. Then on the afternoon of the very same day, we flew a very low altitude test calibrating a new radar altimeter. Believe it or not, we flew from 50 feet above the ground to 500 ft above the ground at speeds up to 400 knots. We began the tests about 12 miles from the range cameras almost flying through the cactus plants! You can't bank the B-52 much when you are only 50 ft above the ground! So Dale and I worked pretty hard that day. The next day, we had to repeat the high altitude tests because we lost three engines in the turns while in buffet on the first day.

I can't remember exactly when we went to Wright Patterson to get our pressure suits fitted, but it had to be before March 1960. I remember we tested them to 75,000 ft in their high altitude pressure chamber though. The suits were very uncomfortable, but they worked, because the blood boils at altitudes of 60,000 ft or more without them. We wore thermal underwear under the suit. Some other interesting facts about these suits were; it took us a good hour to get suited up with the help of a couple of men, and another hour to get it off after the flight still with the men's help. Another amusing fact was if you had to bail out at high altitude, you had to free fall to 15,000 ft before the chute opened automatically. The reason for this was you would freeze to death floating down too slowly at that high of an altitude. (The bad part of all of this was it left black and blue bruise marks on my shoulders and back which caused Cynda to accuse me of having hickies from some extra marital affair, I tried to explain this to her but she didn't believe me.)

During this same time Dale and I were also flying low level terrain following tests on the B-52. We flew 1000-mile legs across the flat lands, through the Rockies, and all over the country. These tests were done to develop a radar system for following the terrain at 200 ft to 400 ft off the ground. We were doing tests to perfect procedures for navigating at those low altitudes. It was rough work because the turbulence at that altitude really shook us around.

From that point on I was doing testing for refueling for both the B-47 and B-52. Structural tests began on the B-52H with Jim Goodell as pilot and again I was the co-pilot. We did the flutter tests on the B-52H with Skybolt Missiles. These seasoned pilots, Dale and Jim, taught me a great deal of respect for those jet giants of the sky. They were also very professional in their work which gave me a leg-up in knowledge later in my life.

B-52 FLUTTER TESTS WITH SKYBOLT MISSILES

Simultaneously at this same period I was flying the F-101B for special tests of the B-52 tail turret radar. In fact you might say I was very busy flying and current in the B-52H, G, D, F; ERB-47E; F-86F, F-100, F-101B and the T-33. I was still flying with the Kansas Air National Guard (KANG) and for a couple of years I flew seven different airplanes. Currency is the matter of your imagination, if you think you're current. Flying all those different airplanes can be very tricky and fatal if you depend on your memory.

I had to develop a habit along the line of refreshing my memory depending on which cockpit I was sitting in. I would go out to the airplane and I would take the checklist and sit down in the cockpit and go over the list and review the location of switches and things before I launched. I don't know how many other pilots do that but I felt like I'd be a little more comfortable if I did. You could really get yourself in trouble if you didn't because we had the F-100C and the F-100D. The C did not have flaps, but the D model had flaps, so consequently there was quite a difference in their landing speed and that mistake could be fatal. My friend Skip Hickey told me (later in life) that was why I was silver haired. The comment was significant to those who never lived to have grey hair.

While all of this flying business was going on, at home we were about to have our second baby. Our little girl Heather had just turned two and Cynda was about to give birth. Her parents owned and operated Smith's Grocery in

Potwin, Kansas, which was about 30 miles east of Wichita where we lived. Her Mom was a good help when we needed her even though she worked all the time in the market. Cynda's sister, Joann and her husband, Raymond, also lived in Potwin. They were a close family who helped take care of our baby girl Heather during the birth of Rich. After a very hard delivery of twenty-three hours, Rich was born January 18, 1961, weighing in at 8 lbs. 1 oz. and 21 ½ inches long! Complications followed the next twenty-four hours into three days. He was having convulsions caused by cerebral hemorrhaging and we rushed him back to the hospital for immediate surgery into the soft spot on his skull and needle suction of the spinal fluid from the base of the spine. Luckily there was a baby specialist at the hospital teaching the very procedure that Richie needed. The doctor was from the Columbia University Hospital of New York.

We brought our baby boy home from the hospital three days later and the doctor told Cynda, "You will have to watch your baby boy round-the-clock to make sure he doesn't have any more seizures!"

It was then Boeing decided to send me and our B-52 flight crew on a refueling mission to Minot, Minnesota. The weather in Wichita had been very icy with snow on the ground. That inclement weather followed us and it started snowing so heavily that we had to abort the refueling mission and were grounded for two days in Minot, Minnesota. This left Grandma Smith taking care of Heather and Cynda at home with our new baby boy only six days old under her constant watch for a recurring seizure. Luckily, Richie never had any more seizures and proceeded to be a very smart little boy. We watched every move he made and finally were convinced he was going to be normal.

So with all of this going on, Boeing selected me to go to the Navy Test Pilot School in Patuxent River, Maryland. This was a big merit badge, you might say. They were preparing me for the Boeing TFX (F-111) flight test program. That gave me a real feel for their confidence in me and I didn't want to disappoint them. Since I would not be able to do my regular duties with the Kansas Air National Guard, I resigned from KANG as Captain. That was August, 1961.

Excited and enthusiastic about this new adventure, we packed our bags and headed for the unknown. It would be even more difficult.

CHAPTER 10

THE NAVY TEST PILOT SCHOOL (TPS)

PATUXENT RIVER, MARYLAND

✦

Our first problem when we got to Patuxent River was finding a place to live. Pre-war housing was barely livable. Living in base quarters was not available to civilians going to the test pilot school. Buying a house in Town Creek was too expensive for us as we were only going to be there during the school term. The military families were assigned for more than a year and had priority on everything, which was as it should be. Solomon Island was a great place too, but it took too long to get from point A to point B. Leonard Town was another little outtake but I needed to be closer to school.

My first week at school was very exciting as we were shown around the facilities and told just what we were going to be experiencing. The director of the school would be having a class party to get the group acquainted. After meeting my new classmates, I imagined Class 31 would be setting a record for firsts at the school, a thought I couldn't get out of my mind.

Cynda and I finally decided to rent a two story pre-war house in Lexington Park. She was not totally enthralled as the place was filthy and we had two little ones, Heather only two and a half, and Richie, eight months. Of course, I had no time to help clean anything as I was starting school almost immediately. The curriculum was going to be severe and with things at home being inconvenient, it would be tough on all of us.

It was September 1961, our class consisted of 16 guys, but there were only 12 golden boys ready and willing to do whatever it took to be the best test pilots in the world. Well actually the representation went sort of like this, Navy – ten, Marines – three, civilian contractors (only one test pilot, me) – three. With a score like this the Navy was sure to win. The fact that I was a contractor pilot, not military, gave me a little bit of an underdog feeling, but not because of any treatment from my military classmates. After all, Boeing was counting on my expertise; as the test pilot is the best instrument a company will ever put in an airplane and certainly the most complicated. I just couldn't let them down. Patuxent River had the reputation of delivering the most professional test pilots in the business, in other words 'the best of the best'.

The complexity of the tests we pilots would be asked to perform, and then write a report on, were a world apart from the normal every day test flying I had been doing. And I realized the next few months would be the most severe challenge of my life…one I did not want to fail. Writing exact reports of 'how' the airplane performed, and precisely 'why' it did or did not perform and 'what' its characteristics were was another frustration for me. The need to put my airplane into every conceivable kind of maneuver and recover it safely, then coordinate and write a record of the total consequences during the test became my worst nightmare. I could probably have told it better, but for some reason writing it out never seemed to feel adequate. However, I realized later in my professional career this phase of the school was extremely helpful in communicating with the engineers I was working with.

The Director of the Test Pilot School was Captain Leo Krupp, a rather reserved guy who was liked by all and would eventually be involved with the astronaut program in Houston. At mid term we got Captain Doug Birdsall, a tall slim dude who knew how to enjoy himself, but certainly was a no-nonsense guy as far as the school was concerned. It was going to be a 'crash' course in a short time; however the object was not to crash! Personalities in that little group were from every aspect of the aerospace scene. Not all were the royal cream of the crop, but most lucked out to graduate including me.

There is one thing I must report; and that is the camaraderie established between friends, in times like these last a lifetime. Even though our noses were held to the grindstone most of the time, we still made Friday nights at Rue's Roost our weekly hangout. The booze flowed freely and the jokes got rather bawdy. The laughter and partying was so infectious that almost all made it to those weekly fetes.

During those first weeks, Director Leo Krupp also introduced himself to our wives with a tour of the school and a private conversation with them. He showed them everything he could about the school including the 'poopy suit' room. This was a room where rubber suits with attached boots hung from the ceiling by the boots, a rather strange looking sight and as I remember for Cynda, kind of a shock. The suits were worn with thermal underwear under them. They were required for survival whenever the Atlantic sea water was below 56 degrees. He told them that these suits were what the pilots had to wear to keep them from hypothermia if they crashed into the Atlantic. The PAX runway was a long narrow strip on the peninsula near the water's edge and if you went into the Atlantic without the suit, well you probably wouldn't survive for long. I think he made it a little more impressive than I have reported here; it got their attention at the time.

There was one other warning which most of the women didn't really pay too much attention to. And that was that a lot of the wives at Patuxent River, if they weren't very careful, would get pregnant! There was talk that something was in the water. Yeh, we all knew it had something to do with school. Would you believe it, nine wives out of the fifteen guys married, sure enough got pregnant. Cynda was one of them.

Things got seriously tougher at home, with a couple of kids under the age of three. She had a very inconvenient house where she washed laundry in a basement; and carried diapers upstairs from there to the line in the yard to hang them to dry. There was only one bathroom on the second floor which was available to her by going through the entire house to get to the stairs to go to the second floor. Those first few weeks of morning sickness really played havoc with my studying and getting my reports in on time; since Cynda had been typing my reports and was too ill to do that anymore.

Mom and Dad Thomas, who lived in Mayville, New York, were about a day's drive from Patuxent River. Now when Mom found out how sick Cynda was, she took the initiative to come and get her and our two kids. So for about four weeks, I was relieved of home problems and could get back on schedule. I had to hire a typist to do my reports, but that worked out okay. Cynda didn't fare as well as she had to put up with my Dad, and he was no easy personality to deal with, especially if you were tossing your cookies every couple of hours.

Back at school, I was getting acquainted with my classmates. I have to say there were about five or six of those guys who really got my attention. I knew from the beginning this experience was going to have a life-long impact on me. As we began to get serious about our studies, personalities began to surface and this group of guys was very talented. We needed to come up with a motto and emblem for our Class 31.

There's a good story about how we came to get the motto "There's A Harder Way". We had a great instructor named, Tom Moore, he was always giving us equations on the board that seemed impossible to factor. Almost every student in our class had a degree in something. I think it was impossible to get into the school without a degree of some kind. Therefore, several of these students could get a little testy in class challenging Tom.

It was on one of these occasions that Instructor Moore proposed an algorithm on the board that left most of the class in a quandary about the hypothesis. So the story goes it was in Tom's Dynamic Stability class that we were examining the solution to a problem he had given us the night before. Roger Box had worked the problem using fifteen or sixteen separate steps to get the answer. Tom went to the blackboard and did it in 'two steps'.

Roger immediately said, "There's a harder way to do that". And "There's A Harder Way" became our class motto.

The Omega symbol had a similar origin. Tom was showing us the mathematical derivation of some flying qualities. He used the Greek symbol Omega for the attribute we were solving. The next day he was reviewing the same solution for us, but this time he used Alpha for the same attribute we were solving. The whole class was befuddled and finally Don Bowen recognized that Alpha was in fact the same thing that was represented the day before by Omega.

With that, Don blurted out, "Yesterday you said that was Omega. How come it is Alpha today?"

So Tom erased the Alphas and replaced them with Omegas and countered, "OK if that is what you want they are Omegas."

Thus the Omega became the center piece of our class emblem. We were a bunch of devoted pilots with enthusiasm for anything that had to do with the school.

♦   ♦   ♦

During the time Cynda was gone to New York with my parents, the next class was just coming on board. Class 32 was about to see how wonderful Class 31 was, as our class would be hosting their "You'll Be Sorry Party". It will be difficult to describe it, but I'll give it a try.

The "You'll Be Sorry Party" is given by the class that is half way through the course. The invitees are the Test Pilot School staff, the new class coming in, and the most recent graduates. The origin of the name refers to the fact that individuals must volunteer to attend the school before they can be selected; hence, 'you'll be sorry' you ever volunteered for this rigorous education. Many long hours of class room work and test flights, data reduction, report writing and study, study, study were required to graduate the course. For Dick Adams and Dick Hoffman, it was rather easy, since they both had a master's degree.

I'm not sure who the gals were that got the ideas together but, they sent out invitations and the dress code would be coat and tie for the men. That meant semi-formal for the women. But, our Class 31's men and women all wore orange flight suits…except for the girls at the reception table outside the main area. They were dressed semi-formal so as not to give away our class 'costumes'.

Upon arrival, each attendee was given a foot long straw with which to imbibe the beverages. Inside the party area, there were four tables with large punch bowls (no glasses). The drinks were labeled Saw Tooth Climb, W over Delta, Rate of Roll, and Lat-Dir. These were tests that we did and wrote reports on. There were Rum, Gin, Vodka and Bourbon drinks. I don't recall the specifics. There was no hors d'oeurves offered at this time…Ahem! To get the crowd loosened up.

After about an hour and a half of socializing, Dick Adam's wife, Wynn, put on her leather jacket and leather helmet becoming Amelia Crashcup. She then joined Smoke Wilson outside on the patio. He had changed into a bright red flight suit, helmet and goggles, with a flowing white scarf around his neck to become Clyde Crashcup! With all the appropriate fanfare, the patio doors opened and he drove his little red Datsun convertible into the Officer's Club. As planned when they opened the car doors to exit, beer cans rolled out onto the floor and Smoke proceeded to do his best impersonation of an inebriated Dean Martin!

The attendees were invited into the adjacent room where we had seating, a small stage, and a movie screen. Carl Dubac, Smoke Wilson and Don Bowen had made several trips to the Naval Photographic Lab at Anacostia, VA. There they reviewed a whole bunch of old films, spliced our 'out takes' together and created the film "This Is Your Life Clyde & Amelia". There was some background music with narration by Don Bowen. Don was so damned funny at times; he would throw us all into fits of laughter. There were shots of WWI and WWII airplanes, and the description of our living accommodations was some shots of Army huts on Attu, Alaska during WWII. The skit was well received. We finally fed the attendees. Our party was talked about from many sources for years afterward. Face it; Class 31 was primed to be either famous or infamous!

I think it is appropriate to say that most all of the wives were completely dedicated to their test pilot husbands and very proud to be part of this frenzied life. They loved their husbands and became caught up in the adrenalin game. This was a time in life like no other, the mystery of the unknown, living unrestrained on a full scope of danger in the sky, playing just as hard at partying and making love. I believe the term is called 'laisser-faire' live and let live for tomorrow you may die. When I think back on that time now, I wonder how I was so lucky to be a part of it all. There is one thing I must add here; Cynda, pregnant and sick, missed the party being at my parents in New York State. I never heard the last of it!

When it came to partying, there were no limits. Rue's Roost was the historical bar hangout in Lexington Park. Each class that came through the school soon found out where to go. You might say the PAX Navy Base essentially owned it. Here almost every test pilot passed through it's portals to boast of his accomplishments. Each of these guys, whether famous astronauts or just plain nobodies, came to see and be seen. Memorabilia of the 'Who's Who's' hung from the rafters of those who had made their mark in aviation history. Walls were plastered with pictures and other unforgettable icons were positioned for posterity…truly an aeronautical museum in its own right.

It was here in these hallowed walls that I, Dick Thomas, sat on the bar and told my joke of the 'Bull and the Bugle' to the graduating Class of 81, at our Class 31's 25th reunion. During the year of our own active class, it wasn't unusual for me to tell this and several other jokes at our class parties. Someone would always goad me into it after a couple of drinks. Now this joke wasn't raunchy like some of my jokes, but it played on a person's capability to portray an old farmer with a speech impediment. So… in my most nasally and tongue-tied speech I started to set the scene… "Well, I owned a prize bull that cost $10,000. One day this fellow from the area knocked on my door. He was trying to convince me to vote for a man running for a political office. I asked him if this was the same man that used to be the operator of the drawbridge at the river. The canvasser said he was the same guy and when I heard that, I sure told him why I wouldn't vote for his candidate…… Well, I had this outstanding bull, you see, and one day when I went into the pasture I found him flat on his back with all four feet sticking straight in the air. His stomach was all bloated and his eyes were rolled back in his head. I was scared I was going to loose my $10,000 prize bull. I called the vet and he told me to get a tub of warm soapy water, a funnel and a hose. Then he said to stick the funnel into the bull's behind, put the hose into the funnel, and siphon the warm soapy water into the bull's stomach. The bull would pass gas and be just fine. Well I started looking for a funnel and I couldn't find one.

But I found my old bugle and I thought this will work just fine, then I couldn't find a hose, but I found an old pitcher and I thought I can pour the warm soapy water into the bugle just fine. So I fixed the warm soapy water in the tub and continued on with this procedure. As I was about half way through giving the bull this treatment, all of a sudden his eyes rolled wide open, he jumped up and passed gas. Well, when he did, it blew that bugle and it scared him so much he started running and jumping all over the place and every time he hit the ground he passed gas and blew that bugle. He kept running down the road and me running after him and when he came to the drawbridge and started to cross it, he was passing gas and blowing the bugle. Well that damned drawbridge operator raised the drawbridge and my $10,000 prize bull fell off the bridge right into the water and drowned. And I wouldn't vote for any dumb son-of-bitch that couldn't tell a ship's horn from a bull with a bugle up his ass!"

This brought down the house at the Roost and the Class 81 participants loved it. There were three of us that got into the joke telling mode at the parties. Roger and Don had their favorites too, acting them out with remarkable applause. Carl was our camera man taking us all on his camcorder, and as we got older, we could see what clowns we made of ourselves. I could see Cynda in these films and she was so embarrassed she was about to squirm out of her chair, as I told my joke. But as I look back, I had to realize what great friends we were and our camaraderie never faded.

Even though my last reunion was not my best as I had been diagnosed with Parkinson's, I attempted the joke; and I may have left some things out. When I finished, the class had put their hearts and heads together and presented me with a wooden plaque. It was appropriately decorated with a brass bull's head and bugle. Two brass plates were engraved with the following: "The Bull and The Bugle, Get Da Bag, Trap Door and The Hag, Thanks for the Laughs". The second plaque read: "To Dick Thomas in remembrance of his performance at the Roost, 1 May 1982, Class 81 loved it". Looking back, this group was the best. I valued their friendship always.

Now as I reminisce about those times and the events that I experienced in those days at PAX River, I felt blessed. The number of remarkable men in my class enlightened me to a perceptive discovery; that I had been plucked from the quagmire of struggling test pilots and dropped into a pool of propitious talent and opportunity. I was especially impressed with their backgrounds. For our class's Outstanding Student at the end of the term, it was none other than Commander Richard Adams, who had graduated from the U.S. Naval Academy at Annapolis, Maryland, then obtained his Master's Degree in Aeronautical Engineering from Princeton. Other 'Who's Who's' in our class that also graduated from the U.S. Naval Academy were Commander Richard Hoffman, Lt. John(Smoke) Wilson, Lt. Roger Box, Lt. Don Lillienthal (all Navy types) and Captain Don Bowen (Marine). I was so charged to be put in a group of elite guys like these; I believed I had won the Golden Fleece Award. After all, Boeing was paying the Navy $50,000 for me to go through the Navy Test Pilot School. That was a heck of a lot of money in my mind as I was only making about $10,000 per year, if that.

CLASS 31 GRADUATES OF PAX TEST PILOT SCHOOL

Yours truly is standing on the left end of the second row, grinning like the proverbial cheshire cat. There were only fifteen of us that graduated, the rest in the picture were instructors. As you will notice, four were Marines, two civilians and the rest were those proud Navy types.

Reality comes knocking quickly though, and performance means just that. There were lots of challenges happening in a short time and some of the students were only there for the academic courses. The guys who were there for pilot training had great potential to become leaders and most of them did. For starters, Roger Box and Smoke Wilson became two-star Admirals. There were several more I'd like to mention here that were outstanding in my book, Lt. Carl Dubac, Captain John Lane , and Captain Donald Bowen (all Marines). After graduation from Test Pilot School we all went our separate ways, but continued to periodically keep in touch. These five guys were some of my most dedicated friends and the information we exchanged over the social scene kept me entertained for years and years. I can honestly say I loved them all. Here are their stories…after graduation.

Immediately after returning from the trip to the United Kingdom Test Pilot School, the following illustrious pilots were given assignments there at Patuxent River. (Unfortunately, since I was not in the military and Boeing was gearing up for the TFX, a new jet fighter, I was needed in Boeing-Seattle and was not allowed the trip with the other graduates.)

Don Bowen, John Lane and Roger Box were assigned to Weapons Test Directorate, where they participated in the testing of new weapons on new aircraft. They flew the F4, F8, A4, A6, and several support aircraft. After four months there, John joined Carl Dubac in the Service Test Directorate. While John's forte was helicopters, he also flew the F4 Phantom, and became the only Marine that qualified as Plane Commander of the P3 Orion. All totaled, he flew six different helicopters, and 25 fixed wing aircraft. Carl Dubac became the lead project pilot for the initial trials of the A4E and the A6A, doing high altitude engine restart tests, engine out approach landing development, and tests on the J-52 engine. Smoke Wilson went to the Flight Test Directorate, Carrier Suitability Branch, where he participated in the initial carrier trials of the E2A (turboprop), the "one and only" TF8E, and the Mach 2, RA5C. During his tour there he flew 28 other aircraft, including the German F-104G, and made a lot of 'hairy landings'.

Wherever the U.S. puts its nose, the Marines are always the first to be called. During this time Smoke and Roger filled their required 'out of the cockpit' obligations as Aide & Flag Lieutenant, and Assistant Navigator (respectively) for 18 months. Our intrepid Marines went from PAX to NAM…though Smoke and Roger were not far behind.

Bowen had two tours there, flying a total of 345 missions in various aircraft, culminating in his command of an F4 Squadron in combat. John flew 56 missions in the F4 in five months…not bad for a Helo guy. Carl made two trips to Vietnam, racking up 274 missions in the A6, A4, & OV1. Roger and Smoke made three tours with the 'Tonkin Gulf Yacht Club'. Together, they flew 377 missions over 'The North Country'. Both commanded a Fighter Squadron and a Carrier Air Wing.

Who got what is not all that important. The sum is most impressive. In eleven tours, these five guys collected a Legion of Merit, 3 Distinguished Flying Crosses, 2 Bronze Stars, 70 Air Medals, 5 Commendation Medals (for valor), a Navy Achievement Medal, 4 Unit Citations, and 3 Vietnam Gallantry Crosses. Not a bad group. I'm glad they were on our side.

Where'd they go from there? Well, when John came home to El Toro from Vietnam, it became apparent that the Marine Corps was going to send him back to NAM as a helicopter pilot. NOT!!! He resigned his commission and went to work for Douglas Aircraft as a test pilot. He started flying the newest versions of the A4, and went on to do DC9 and DC10 certification work. He flew the YC-15, and then became the Project Pilot on the MD80. McDonnell Douglas Corporation then selected him as their first Chief Experimental Test Pilot. Because of medical problems, he retired from the aerospace industry in 1994.

The next of these guys to depart the 'cloth' was Bowen. He went to Washington, first to NAVAIR in the A7 Program Management Office (where he managed to boondoggle flight time at PAX River), and then to the Pentagon, where he served as the OP NAV coordinator of all USMC Air Armament System Development. In 1972 he passed this responsibility to Carl and he retired in 1974. Don subsequently became a District Marketing Manager for Sundstrand Aerospace.

After his first Vietnam tour, Carl was ordered to the Naval Post Graduate School where he received an MS in Electrical Engineering and then returned to

Vietnam. Upon his return, he served as OIC of the Avionics Department at the USMC Development at the USMC Development Center, Quantico, Virginia until he relieved Don Bowen in OP NAV. Carl served with distinction on the OP NAV billet…a difficult and demanding assignment. During this time his wife was dying of breast cancer. Since his impending assignment was overseas, he chose to stay with his beloved and retired in 1976. In 1977, he founded and subsequently became CEO of a multi-million dollar corporation, named DCS Corporation. Such a deal!

Box and Wilson were the last men standing, and they stood tall. Not surprisingly, their careers were quite similar. They commanded F4 squadrons, and they both commanded an Air Wing. Cynda and I had the privilege of attending their change of command aboard the aircraft carrier USS ENTERPRISE. One truly feels the depth of their sincerity to duty and love of their country when witnessing the 'pomp and circumstance' of this ceremony.

Roger and Smoke consecutively served as the Flight Test Officer at the Naval Missile Center, where they were among the first to fly the F-14 Tomcat. They served in the Weapons Acquisition Group in the Naval Air Systems Command, and both were selected for flag rank while serving as Chief of Staff on Naval Air Force Pacific…this time Smoke relieved Roger. Previously, Roger was the *first* Commanding Officer of the Navy Fighter Weapons School, better known as *TOP GUN*! They both commanded Fleet logistic support ships, and while Roger commanded the carrier USS RANGER. Smoke commanded eight ammunition ships in the Pacific Fleet. Roger attended the U.S. Air Force Command and Staff College, while Smoke attended the Armed Forces Staff College. Roger commanded a Carrier Battle Group in the Mediterranean, served a joint tour with the Supreme Headquarters Allied Powers Europe, and retired from duty as the Director of Operation, U.S. Space Command in March of 1997. Smoke's joint tour was as Director of Logistics and Security Assistance, U.S. Pacific Command. He then became the Commander of the Pacific Missile Test Center…his third tour at Point Mugu. Next was the Naval Air Systems Command, where he served as the Deputy Commander for Systems Engineering. His final assignment was as the Chief of Naval Research. He retired in June of 1990. They both retired as Rear Admirals (two stars). And I remember Smoke telling me he had more than

1,000 carrier arrested landings. He and I both made 'Fellow' status in the Society of Experimental Test Pilots.

It was during one of those times that Commanding Officer Roger Box invited me and several other friends to come aboard as his guests on the aircraft carrier to observe the Navy maneuvers in the Pacific. So from North Island, we were transported by a Navy S2F to the USS RANGER. There, we stayed a couple of days watching the show of the Pacific Fleet. Then it was back to reality again. It was a highlight I have not forgotten over the years. And Roger's ship was the recipient of the Admiral Arleigh Burke Award as the most improved operating unit in the entire Pacific Fleet.As you can see all these guys became super heroes in my book. They were also great joke tellers. Like I said I felt so fortunate to be in their association.

◆   ◆   ◆

Time was slipping by fast; and soon our tour at PAX River would come to an end. Graduation was just about three months off. I found a better house for us down on the peninsula, it was a one story newer place and I thought Cynda would be much better off since she wouldn't have to trot up and down those steep stairs carrying Richie. He was weighing about 26 lbs then and she was about four month's pregnant and really popping out. It was a sight to see her try to carry that big baby with that stomach of hers as she was pretty thin and little.

Well the house didn't work out as well as I had hoped. It seems the builder had just taken a saw and sawed off the thicket trees, then built the little house over the stumps without killing them or putting a pest killer down to rid cockroaches. We moved into the house not knowing it was totally infested with cockroaches from the tree stumps. We had two little people in that house and couldn't leave anything out of the refrigerator that wouldn't be attacked by the roaches.

This was Maryland; thickets of every kind were growing in each direction from the house. If your child wondered off into the thickets you would probably never find them. Heather was three by then and Richie was fourteen months and already running after her wherever she went. There was no place for them to play that wasn't dangerous. The main highway to the peninsula point ran right in front of the house, so letting them out to play in front was out of the question.

The back yard was just as scary because the thickets started at the end of the back yard and there was no fence to stop either of the kids going into the thickets. These were trees of many kinds only six or eight inches apart with a willowy trunk of four to six inches in diameter. So a child could squeeze through them and become lost in no time at all. On top of all that, the ticks were very fierce and the neighbor's dog would go yelping all over the place with large ticks you could actually see on his body. Cynda would go over the kids every night to make sure there were no ticks on them.

I was studying hard, trying to make a decent grade and worrying about her at home. Many nights I would stay at the PAX Navy library and study then get home pretty late. She was afraid out there and I had to admit I didn't do her any favors by moving her there. Then Richie and Heather only had a tiny little room with no doors, it was actually more like a small dining room. We had two baby beds for them and there was just enough room to walk between them. If one woke up and cried then the other one would wake up and cry too. Cynda was constantly getting up to check on them at night as the cockroaches would come out at night and get on the kids. She would almost get hysterical trying to kill cockroaches. We tried everything to get rid of them but they were impossible to get to under the house and nothing seemed to work.

Regardless of all these problems we were confronting, we were having a great time with these new friends. During all this hard work, we also had fun. These military people had a way of creating their own entertainment and it was called "Phantom-ing". Yeh, I know it sounds like a kid's game but once it started it was all that was talked about. Several couples would be out partying and decide they wanted to go see one of the other couples who weren't there, or had left early. It would be either very late at night or early morning hours. In those days no one locked their front door. So, the couples doing the deed would go to the house, walk into the people's bedroom, wake them up, get them out of bed and raid their kitchen for food or whatever. You just never knew what to expect. In reality, everyone involved seemed to take it in their stride, maybe there were a few disgruntled classmates, but most had a good laugh about it all.

Graduation night came and what a night we had celebrating. After months and months of hard studying, we were raring to acknowledge the fact that we had accomplished our goals. Scott and Rene' Carpenter (one of the first astronauts and a graduate of the PAX River Test Pilot school) were guests of our graduating class. Scott was the speaker and darned if I can remember a word he said. But just to have his presence at our graduation was enough. It probably had something to do with the drinks we were all consuming that night.

I had invited my brother Don and his wife Nance to come for the ceremony. We only had one bedroom in that tiny house. Cynda declared we couldn't put them on the fold-out couch in the living room, so we gave them our bed; and we slept on the couch. There was a rousing after-grad party at Rue's Roost and we finally got to bed about 4 a.m. I was pretty bad (meaning drunk), Cynda was in her sixth month pregnancy and very tired. We had just got the kids settled again, after making noise and waking them when we came home. The baby sitter had left and we inadvertently did not lock the screen door when she left.

Then all of a sudden bright beams of car lights were shining in our living room, and the rascals had attacked us. Smoke Wilson drove his very small Datsun convertible filled with graduates and their wives right up to the porch. And a couple other cars followed him across the lawn right up to the front porch also. They unloaded, and were rowdily getting us all up. It was June, 1962, in Maryland, hot and sticky. I was sleeping in my boxer shorts and Cynda had on a red shorty see-through nightgown which was wrong side out (she didn't realize it until they left).

The chaos that followed was unbelievable; being seriously plastered I could have slept on a bed of nails that night. The group really had their fun with me, not that I recalled anything, but Cynda gave me the humiliating details later. No sheet covered us as it was too hot. And when they couldn't wake me, they decorated me with toilet paper and markings! Cynda was too embarrassed to do anything and they woke the kids again then left. This was our life in PAX River and it was about to end. True, we might move away, but the friendships would last forever.

I had graduated from the U. S. Naval Test Pilot School, and while at school, I flew the F-11F, F-J4B, F-4D, T-28, T2V, UF1, and the S-2F. Smoke would tell me later that he was quietly informed that since the F-4D's flying qualities were very squirrely…consequently, he and I were the only ones selected to fly it at the time.

We had one tragedy during that school season, Jim Isca, a Northrop engineer taking the academic course requested to fly during his term there and during a flight in the F-11 had an accident and was killed, leaving a pregnant wife of seven months and six children. This was a very sad state of affairs since he wasn't required to fly anyway.

Finally, it was pack up and get back to Wichita and Boeing. I had conquered the beast here and now I had my work cut out for me as one of the two pilots assigned to fly the first tests on the new fighter, the TFX. Things were looking great, I thought!

I had been to Seattle talking to the Boeing people regarding the TFX. We were all anxiously awaiting the government decision of the contract award. Finally, it came one morning and as we listened and watched the announcement on television. I had a gut wrenching disappointment to learn Boeing did not get the contract award, but it went to General Dynamics, their Convair Division in Ft.Worth, Texas.

We were settled back in our nice little house on Wicker Lane in Wichita. Cynda was getting things ready for the birth of our third baby. It was September, 1962, and production had just ended on the B-52. That same month our PAX baby girl was born, a true Thomas with auburn red hair exactly the same color as my dad's. We named her Velvet Renee.

B-52 experimental testing continued on with terrain following and other systems, but several crews were vying for possible flights. That terrain following was quite interesting. We would fly low level flights following the elevation of the land all over the country. In only a couple of years I'd flown fourteen different types of airplanes and really began to feel that this test flying was not too bad.

Since I was the youngest test pilot in the bunch at Boeing, the other crews found an ad in the Aviation Week for a pilot that was a graduate of test pilot school and had just my experience. I fit the bill perfectly and they persuaded me to send my resume to the company. It wasn't long before I heard from that company. Northrop Corporation wanted to fly me out to California to interview for their job. They would pay for my wife to come also. So out we went.

Cynda's sister, Joann, had moved from the little town of Potwin, Kansas, and lived with her family in Buena Park, CA. They had not seen our beautiful little redhead baby, Velvet. Therefore, the three of us flew out for three reasons, to look the place over, show off our newest creation and for me to interview with Northrop. It was February, 1963. Northrop offered me a job on their new F-5A contract, I reluctantly accepted. I really hated to leave Boeing, they had been so good to me. Was I doing the right thing? But, I needed to go where the action was!

CHAPTER 11

NORTHROP & EDWARDS AIR FORCE BASE

✦

The Vice President & General Manager, Welko Gasich, hired me into Northrop. He had received my resume and had it on his desk when a guy named Tony Bauer happened to be talking to him in his office and noticed my application. Ironically, that Tony Bauer was a roommate of mine in college too! Now is that a coincidence or just lucky, I don't know.

Anyway it seems Tony asked, "Welko are you thinking of hiring this guy?

Gasich answered, "Yes, I'm flying him and his wife out here to interview for the job."

Tony then told him, "Well, we were roommates in college and he's a good guy. I haven't seen him for a while, so I'll contact him and set up a dinner with him."

So fate plays a big part in life even if you don't think so. When we received the tickets from Northrop to fly to Los Angeles, Cynda had been scheduled to have a small cyst removed from the side of her nose. Consequently she had to cancel that minor surgery. During the plane ride to Los Angeles, Velvet, our six-month old baby girl, would not sleep and kept bouncing on Cynda's lap. During one of those bounces, her head hit Cynda in the face bruising the cyst. By the time our important dinner with Northrop people came around, she looked like she had two noses! We were staying with her sister and family at their Buena Park home and the two of them laughed about her 'two noses' till tears rolled down her face. She tried to explain her situation, but there were no words to make up for the embarrassment she felt at that dinner. It didn't matter that I had a wife with 'two noses', they still offered me the job.

Lancaster, California, was a very barren place when we moved here in March of 1963. There were houses boarded up in lots of areas. I think the population was about 13,000 and Palmdale, a neighboring town was 7,000. The main road into town was Sierra Highway; of course it went through the mountains south to Saugus and picked up the better highway there at the four corners. That highway led straight into the beautiful San Fernando Valley with fancy stores like Robinson's, I. Magnin, and Bullocks. Now, forty years later the valley has gone to the 'dogs'. Nothing remains the same and it has become a ghetto for low income, crime ridden mafia type gangs. And unfortunately, our own Antelope Valley has become a victim of spill-over and is showing signs of the same disgraceful circumstance.

Cynda was in for a cultural shock out here in the boon docks again, as she had been used to the bustling city of Wichita, Kansas, with nice shopping. I was not used to driving thirty-plus miles to work either; as we had lived off Rock Road, in Wichita, only a few miles from Boeing. Now we needed two cars; so being the very conservative person that I was--I bought a used white Jaguar convertible that needed a new top! She wasn't impressed.

I remember my first day at Northrop Corporation at Edwards; it felt like I was driving out into the middle of nowhere. I had left Boeing-Wichita and wasn't really sure what I had gotten myself into. Boeing had a clause in their contract that if you quit, you could not come back as a rehire. I wasn't sure if I had made the right choice. I didn't know what I was going to be doing at Northrop/ Edwards. I knew Boeing would have taken care of me financially and given me a good retirement when the time came. But I had read a lot about things going on at Edwards AFB and for some reason I was drawn to the desert to try my luck at the unknown. And, I had been here several times before with the Boeing B-52; and to check out in the F-100 by North American's Chief Pilot, Bob Baker.

Most of the pilots flying at Edwards were breaking the sound barrier. Maybe it was the legend of Chuck Yeager and his historic flight, but regardless, it was too late to turn back. As I pulled up to the security gates, the guard stopped me and checked me for my base ID. I told him I was a new pilot here, but the guard just smiled and said "Good luck buddy you're gonna need it".

I asked him, "What do you mean by that?"

And he razzed me by saying, "Well out at Edwards, pilots are a dime a dozen just like the sand! You'll be just another 'jet jockey'. You're gonna need lots of luck on your side if you expect to distinguish yourself from the rest. Why, there are so many pilots out there, it seems like everybody wants to come to California to be a fly-boy!"

As he waved me on through the gates, he finished his preaching with, "No offense son, but just remember it's the dream a lot of guys have, and this is the place where things are really happening. Hell, they kill three at a time out here!"

I drove off thinking, yeah sometimes the answers are all right in front of us, but we just don't see them. Something had led me to come out to California just like all the other guys, and I knew I wouldn't be the only one with dreams of glory. In my heart I already knew the guard was telling me the true facts. Many of the best pilots were here; they came from all over the place. They came to Edwards because of the myths, the stories, and of course the legends. They all came for the same reasons I did, they wanted to be part of history.

I drove up to the Northrop hangar, parked my white XK6 Jaguar and looked around. I noticed another guy drive up and park about the same time I did. He got out of a white Porsche sports car. Standard uniform for a test pilot, I decided.

He nodded in my direction, "You're new?" he asked.

I looked at him and said, "Yeah I'm the new guy in from Boeing-Wichita, Dick Thomas."

"Hank Chouteau" he stated and stuck his hand out to me.

We shook hands and walked into the office together. He didn't say much but I liked his demeanor right away. I never liked people who talked a lot about a little and never said much. Hank was straight and to the point and talked with purpose. He was a big guy with the walk and enormity of John Wayne. In a word, he was cool, so much so that I felt like I could learn something from him. He was definitely a guy you could trust and when he laughed it was real. He wasn't a kiss-ass or a schmoozer. Hank could walk the walk and talk the talk, no bullshit, which was obvious. He had his beliefs but he wasn't busy telling them to everybody. I felt he was the epitome of a 'hired gun', just a guy who came to work, did his job everyday, even if that job was something as extraordinary as test-flying jets. He would become another one of my close friends.

There was an underlying mystic about the place, from the decaying walls of the Pancho Barnes dilapidated Happy Bottom Riding Club to the echoes of those sound breaking flights across the desert sky. This was the place where anything might happen; at least there was the 'possibility for the potential' something I always told myself and my kids.

Many pilots had the potential, but lacked the opportunity. At Edwards there was always the chance to come in contact with some kind of opportunity. I realized then that this was why I left Boeing, I couldn't see myself sitting at a desk and doing a managerial job hiring young guys to do what I knew I had the capability to do myself. I wanted to take the risk of flying aircraft that no one could predict whether you would live or die. Why I felt like that is anyone's guess, but I had to take that chance of being one of those guys that could achieve something on the cutting edge of aerospace technology.

I guess secretly, all pilots want to make their 'mark' in aerospace, get a little glory, a little prestige, and their fifteen minutes of fame. At the same time, flying those special programs had its good parts too; bonus money was like frosting on the cake. The bigger the thrill, the bigger the bonus too! There are no guarantees in this business, yet I was willing to bet on the odds. Just like so many others, I would become even more of a gambler as I got on in age. But at 33 years old I was still a fighter and as I learned the ropes I knew I would have to fight for my opportunities.

Not long after I was hired into Northrop, I was sent to survival training school. We were taken to remote areas of the mountains and dropped off. We were left to our own devices with a two-way wrist radio for contact with the other ground troops. As night approached we had sleeping bags to pitch and crawl into. As I settled into my sleeping bag for the night, I felt something crawling up my leg. I thought I had heard something that sounded like a rattlesnake and I became fearful that it was in fact a rattlesnake that was crawling on me. I started calling on my wrist radio for the survival group to get them to come and get it off me, but they ignored me. Finally, it crawled up on my shoulder and chest and curled up, as a snake will go to the warmest part of your body I guess to get warm. I kept calling them to come and get it off and they said it wouldn't do any good because it would bite me anyway. I laid there without moving for what seemed like an eternity and finally it crawled off and crawled away.

I never got over that awful scare and Cynda couldn't understand why I had such terrible nightmares of snakes. I was always killing snakes or trying to kick them off me in dreams and she would wake me up and ask what was wrong. During the survival training, we were taught to kill snakes and cook them for eating. Some of the guys were actually dropped into areas that were not civilized and there were a lot of poisonous snakes. I've eaten alligator and snake, they're okay as long as you bite them first, I just got sick of rattlesnake. We made water out of cactus and were trained to hide in order not to be seen by others, find animal burrows and dig in. And you were told to walk your way out! Funny, I can't remember how I got out, but I must have walked my way out--and I always thought I was a tough scout!

As I became better acquainted with Hank Chouteau, I realized he was a guy you could learn a lot from and I asked him about his desire to fly and just how he got into the business. He told me he was working for a construction company after high school graduation. They were building a U.S. Army Air Base at Casper, Wyoming. And, some of his friends wanted to take the examination to become aviation cadets. So they talked him into taking the test with them. As it turned out Hank was the only one that passed the test, but he was only seventeen and couldn't sign up. The Army suggested that they could save the test results and when he turned eighteen they would sign him up. Hank agreed and in August of 1942, he was sworn into the Army as an Aviation Cadet.

He was called to active duty in February, 1943 and completed his training in March, 1944. Stationed in Europe with the 9th Air Force, Hank flew combat missions in the B-26 Martin Marauder against German targets from France. When the war ended he was in line to be returned to the United States and consequently reassigned to Nordholtz, Germany, to the U.S. Army Air Base there. The 121st U.S. Army Airbase Hospital was based in Bremerhaven about twenty minutes from his base. There was a nurse stationed there named Bettieann Mays that would become the future Mrs. Chouteau.

Hank was a very valuable supporter on my behalf and he was also a fighter for the test pilots as a group. He flew the first flight of the F-5A and many of the first flights on subsequent F-5's. My first check out at Northrop was in the T-38 Talon, a very nice little jet trainer. Finally in September of 1963 I got my checkout in the F-5A. I brought in the F-5 prototype that started out as an N-156 and became the YF-5A. I was doing the first gun firing tests of the F-5A day and night. Then I started doing flutter testing, stability and control tests, and finally store separation (bomb) drops. I had some rather hairy moments with one of those bomb drops later on.

It was about this time Hank talked me into joining the SETP, Society of Experimental Test Pilots. The headquarters were in Lancaster and several large aerospace corporations had factories in the Antelope Valley. It is really interesting to join a group of fellows that you have heard their names mentioned over aerospace rhetoric. But, to walk into the room where they are gathered in jovial conversation and know you are one of them, is the best reward of all. I was an immediate fan of the organizational group. In my time, my name would be added to their list of awards.

Then in March of 1964 the X-21 Laminar Flow Control airplane was the first weird bird I would be testing, and I was designated the Project Pilot. At that time they were allowing test pilots to fly multiple airplanes. This was a big exotic airplane. This rather strange looking duck was a converted B-66 weather airplane with laminar flow control on the wings so that it had miles of slots on the wings.

THE X-21 LAMINAR FLOW TEST BED

In 2000, I was interviewed by Major Ruth Williamson, USAFR, in Dayton. 'Skip' Hickey had arranged for this meeting at the request of the historical group at the Wright-Patterson Air Force Museum. Cynda and I were there for the 2000 Stealth Pioneer Awards Banquet. Later on that evening I was presented with my own Stealth Pioneer Award plaque, a complete surprise. Skip had alerted Cynda in order to be sure to get me there. Skip and I had become friends since he worked on special projects as a government engineer. In 1964 the Northrop X-21 was Skip's first airplane to work on for the government, and a lot of friendly bantering went on between us at this reunion. Skip had also worked on my last Northrop project, the Tacit Blue in 1982.

Did I say the X-21 was a very weird looking airplane? First it had a rather large hump on its back. It also had very squirrelly characteristics. There were pumping pods under the wings to suck the boundary layer off the wing; and it had aft-mounted engines. Therefore it was a big change in the airplane that made it have nasty stall tendencies. I never had it happen to me, but I know that if you used too much fuel out of the forward tank it would taxi with the nose wheel lifting off the ground! So during the interview, I am telling this story to the Major and…

At this point, Major Ruthie interrupts asking, "Porpoise?"

I answered, "Yes…coming off the ground!"

She laughed, "Yes, great!"

"Something you don't often do! Was this design theory your fault, Skip?" I asked, we all laughed.

Skip interjected, "No, not me. I was just a GS-5 at the time."

There were a couple other stories I can recall that were significant with the X-21. This was probably the most boring airplane to fly that I had ever flown. Reason being, you would take off from Edwards AFB and after reaching your set altitude fly as straight as you could as far north as the gas would take you, make only one turn and fly straight back to base, all this over a period of three to four hours. The engineers would be down in the airplane belly working the data as fast as they could.

On one of these occasions as Don Murray, the engineer tells it, he and Roy Whites, the Chief Engineer, were sitting behind me. I had my headphones on and just sitting there relaxed watching the world go by. Roy Whites had a question and yells up to me--and I do not respond at all. Then he asks Don Murray if I am all right?

At that point, Don leans up and pokes my arm to get my attention and yells, "Hey Dick, are you OK?"

With that move, I lift my earphones and respond, "Oh yeah, I had the radio set on ADF just listening to Dick Whittinghill on KMPC; and I was thinking how cool it would be to give Whittinghill the Reno traffic report as we flew over!"

Don told me later that he almost strangled to keep from laughing. For those of you who might not know who Whittinghill was, he had a great reputation in the Los Angeles area as the funniest DJ going. His quips about 'around the corner and up her street, reaching for her knocker' were famous and most of the time hilarious, with serious innuendos on the naughty side.

That didn't go over too well. Then on another occasion Lew Nelson, my boss and chief pilot at the time decided he was going to fly the X-21. Now Lew was not my biggest fan and certainly had his reasons for that I'm sure. The cockpit and console of the X-21 were very wide and I had about six inches of reach (and maybe height) more than Lew. But, there were several areas of the cockpit panel that required reaching in both directions simultaneously. So on the day Lew came out to the airplane to tell me he was going to fly it, instead of me. I inadvertently spouted off, "Hell Lew, you're too short to fly this plane."

He would prove me wrong. He did fly; but red-faced and utterly enraged, he whirled and stamped back towards the hangar. With that statement sealing my fate, I knew time might be rather short too, in this job. It was to come back and bite me later.

Life got rather serious after these two rather stupid moves on my part. On an early 4 a.m. phone call from Spain in 1964, I learned just how serious this business was. As I answered that call, it was the sad news that a fellow Northrop test pilot had been killed during a sales demonstration show in the F-5. Don Papish, a talented pilot, had allowed a rather heavy Spanish officer to fly in the rear cockpit for this demonstration. During this sales show, he was scheduled to do a Cuban eight maneuver. And as Don came into the second section of the Cuban eight, he started his roll from inverted to upright; then pointed the nose into the dive. At this point his descent to a safe altitude became too difficult to pull out of because the Spanish officer's portly body was, in fact, pushing against the stick and Don could not pull out of the dive. They needed about ten more feet of ground clearance. The tail impacted the ground with the aircraft descending in a nose-high altitude. The aircraft then pitched over, nose striking the ground, exploded and disintegrated. Consequently they were both killed in the crash, while the Spanish officials and guests looked on in horror. Both of them left wives and children.

According to the engineers, everything they asked me to do was 'a simple test'. I was doing the first gun firing tests of the F-5A day and night. Then there were stability and control tests, flutter tests and store (bomb) drops. As I stated, it was a simple test or at least that was what it started out to be, on that beautiful day on the edge of the Mojave Desert. As I was finishing my tests and coming back for my landing, on final approach I inadvertently hit the stores red button, releasing two dumb bombs in the 'General's back yard' (figuratively speaking).

The F-5 had a very tight cockpit and they were always looking for a place to add another button or instrument. So those intelligent engineers decided to put the stores red button on the stick next to the black radio call button. I think I was probably set up now that I wonder about the placement, but at any rate, this fiasco would haunt me for about six months. But I set the story straight at my retirement party. I'll give you a full disclosure of the real stuff then.

I had survived all my serious blunderings and decided life might settle down. Things were going along pretty normal now I thought, until November 4th, 1965. And from a better source than my memory, I will just copy my article published in the Society of Experimental Test Pilots Cockpit magazine. So here goes…

"Ejection Over the High Sierras"
By R. G. Thomas

Unfortunately, the lead-in events of this escapade started just like the trite old Hollywood opening, "There I was flat on my back over Mt. Whitney at 34,000 feet hanging by my straps."

The F-5A flight started as a normal maintenance and instrumentation check-out on November 4, 1965, and ended due to an uncontrollable rolling condition following inverted flight. The results of the accident investigation have not been released. But for this narration, cause is important only in its direct influence on the conditions during ejection and the time available to evaluate the problem.

The initial conditions were set just following supersonic flight to 1.4 IMN (indicated MACH number) when the airplane was slowed to 200 KIAS (knots indicated air speed) and rolled to inverted flight. During the roll-out from inverted flight the airplane continued to roll past the upright level flight attitude and kept on rolling with the nose dropping lower on each roll. As near as we have been able to re-construct the flight, it took approximately one minute from roll-out until the airplane contacted the ground in a vertical attitude at greater than MACH 1.

Following the first few rolls, I called the flight test ground personnel and advised them that I would probably leave the airplane due to loss of control. They nonchalantly "rogered" my call and then realized what I had said. This call immediately alerted everyone who had a listening watch on the test frequency, particularly Edwards Approach Control. I followed my first call with a second (last) to inform them of my position, which was very nearly over Mt. Whitney (14,000 feet elevation). And to confirm the fact that I was going to eject. I actually related my position to Owens Dry Lake, since I could see it once each revolution.

The airplane transitioned from level flight at 300 KIAS to 70 degrees nose down and 375 KIAS during the period of time it took to complete the two radio calls. While this was taking place, opposite aileron was used to slow the roll rate, but I was never able to reduce the roll rate much below 300°/sec., even with maximum rudder coordinated with aileron against the roll. With the control stick released, the roll rate appeared to be about 350°/sec. I tried but was unsuccessful in coordinating aft stick with roll attitude in an attempt to raise the nose above the horizon. After a couple of attempts at this maneuver the procedure was rejected, since the high roll rate made coordination very difficult. At the time I thought I might be able to improve ejection conditions with this maneuver or at least get over the Owens Valley, but it was obvious that I was stuck with a high roll rate every time I let go of the stick.

The final radio call and decision to eject was made at 25,000 feet. The airplane was rolling at approximately 360°/sec., with 375 KIAS at 23,000 feet when I got everything pulled. The calculated rate of descent at ejection was 30,000 feet/minute over terrain of 11,000 feet elevation. I made no attempt to get in the classic ejection posture other than placing my arms firmly in the arm rests prior to initiating ejection, due to the haste required at that point. The seat has automatic leg and calf protection so I did not suffer any injuries at this time; however, it appears that the wind blast slammed my head against the headrest. The helmet had the paint cracked on the right rear side as though struck by a blunt instrument. This probably accounted for my being dazed until chute deployment. The seat was a standard Northrop rocket seat with sequencing such that squeezing the trigger starts all actions automatically in proper order. This seat has automatic man/seat separation, auto lap belt, and chute deployment. The rest of my equipment consisted of a summer flying suit, leather boots, Northrop emergency radio beacon, and a standard Air Force back pack with a 28-foot diameter canopy. The seat sequence appeared to work properly, but following canopy and seat separation from the airplane, I was unaware of the action until the chute opened. The opening shock or wind blast took my right glove off which caused problems during descent. Since I was over the High Sierras at the time of ejection, it appeared, at first that I would land very high up on Mt. Whitney, so I started side-slipping the chute towards the Owens Valley. After a few minutes of pulling on the risers my right hand became so cold I had to put it between my legs to prevent frost bite.

The rest of the descent was uneventful probably because there was no surface wind and the temperature on the valley floor was approximately seventy degrees Fahrenheit. There did appear to be some up-draft which slowed my initial descent but landing was calculated to be at approximately 33 feet/sec. The landing was at the 8,000-foot level on the northeast side of Mt. Whitney about seven and one-half miles southwest of Lone Pine, California. This area is primarily boulders and deep gullies, with the boulders being the approximate size of automobiles or larger. Due to the nature of the terrain, no attempt was made to precisely control the landing spot.

An attempt was made to assume the correct landing position and contact was made on top of a large boulder with both feet together and knees slightly bent. Even though both knees were twisted severely at touch down due to the hard surface, the correct position probably prevented leg fractures. My helmet and mask stayed on during the entire ejection and landing, probably due to the tight fit which I have tried to maintain. The helmet was a Lombard with a Hardman retaining kit and an A-15 Air Force mask. My visor was up during the proceedings and, as a result of this, I acquired a black eye from an unidentified blow during the ejection or chute opening.

As soon as I recovered from the landing shock I began to wonder how I was going to get down the rest of the way. The automatic antenna on my emergency beacon was broken and I did not think about getting the spare out. At this time I noticed another F-5A making passes up and down the valley…below my present altitude of 8,000 feet. This turned out to be another Northrop pilot, Hank Chouteau, who was trying to see if I was near the wreckage. He never got high enough to see me wave or see my chute on the ground, since he was making his passes at about 6,500 feet. After the initial search airplanes left the area, I decided I would have to walk down. By this time, I spotted a house a couple of miles away and figured a telephone call was the best means of contact.

With everything gathered up into a pack I started following the dry washes down to a lower elevation. I had walked down to about the 5,500-foot level when Lt.Col. Jesse Jacobs came by in a C-130. They spotted me on the second pass after I started a brush fire and a few minutes behind Jesse came an H-21 helicopter, piloted by Capt. Dave Thomas. I had been out of the airplane about two hours when the H-21 picked me up. (The rapid response turned out to be another item of luck from a long list in my favor. The C-130's were returning from an XB-70 support mission and diverted to the area prior to reaching Edwards AFB.)

Considering the conditions, my injuries were minor and limited to bruises from the chute opening, and bruises and abrasions from landing in the boulders along with two wrenched knees. I think the results of this ejection over terrain and conditions, much different from the departure airport; point up the need for having the appropriate survival gear available at all times. Another point which seems to trap many pilots, particularly test pilots, is staying with the airplane too long. A timely decision is one of the most important factors for ejection survival.

The radio call of my position helped in the search and I feel it was very worthwhile; however, Edwards Approach was able to establish a close fix from reports of various observers in the area. A deer hunter in the area spied me and my parachute coming down and phoned the Edwards Air Force Base headquarters my approximate location. Other observers also called military and official government personnel.

MY LUCKY PARACHUTE NO. 13

After the helicopter deposited me back to base, I had a quick checkout at the Edwards AFB hospital. Then Northrop delivered me home to Lancaster with one of the Northrop engineers driving my car. Cynda had quickly been alerted of the ejection by Bettieann Chouteau. Shortly word spread through Lancaster that Dick Thomas had ejected over Mt. Whitney. No one knew at that time whether I was alive or dead. After several hours of panic, Cynda was relieved to know I was alive, but still no news of the details of the crash, my circumstances or condition. So when I arrived home, neighbors and friends filled the house. It was very difficult to walk, as both knees and legs were swollen and sprained. I was immediately put to bed with a couple of pills the Edwards doctor had prescribed. After Cynda put me to bed, our three kids arrived from the nursery school and came to rescue poor old dad and see if I was alright.

The night was one horrible nightmare and Cynda said, "Honey, you moaned and groaned all night. I tried to wake you and you just moaned more!"

I stayed home for the next two days in bed, the swelling in my legs was almost gone and even though my knees were weak and hurting, I managed to go to work the next day. It was necessary to have physical therapy on my knees for about six months, but I didn't tell anyone at work because I didn't want to be grounded. Well, I guess I walked good enough to fool them. I was back in the cockpit three days later! In those days at Edwards, pilots were getting killed three at a time it seemed and I had to feel very lucky that I hadn't become a statistic.

During the accident investigation, it was discovered that the aileron actuator failed in the F-5, thus shutting down F-5 operations until corrective action could be taken on any F-5's in service around the world. Whether it was FOD (foreign object damage) that made it fail or the part itself, no one ever told me. You might say, these past two years with Northrop were peppered with rather negative incidents of 'bad luck'; or you could say that 'Dick Thomas' has been on a learning curve, and just maybe around the corner he would come back with a vengeance of 'good luck'.

Aerospace was slowing down at Northrop and there was a lot of politics going on in the flight department. I was not in the best of good graces with some of the management. There was that feeling of being pushed from pillar to post; and even though I thought I was doing my best to do the job, certain people didn't like me. I was trying hard to keep my spirits up and I had applied for the astronaut program with people from Northrop backing me. During this time I had met several of the astronauts as they were being checked out in Northrop's T-38 jet trainer.

In 1964, the astronauts needed airplanes to stay 'current' in and be proficient, so they were sending Neil Armstrong to evaluate the T-38. Neil was from the Antelope Valley and I had met him a few times before he became an astronaut. Neil and I flew a T-38 to Houston; Neil was in the back seat and I was flying so he could evaluate the airplane. When we landed, NASA had a photographer on hand to take pictures. Neil had not been to the moon yet, but he was in line. It was very interesting to me because of the people involved. We were instructed to fly into Tinker Air Force Base at Enid, Oklahoma, from Houston. Why they picked Enid, I don't know. However, the base had very little air traffic and terrain was very flat there. So it probably had something to do with safety factor.

The astronauts that were going to fly the T-38 were picked up in Houston and then flown to Enid for landing. On my first stop the tower got pretty uppity with me 'cause they thought I was taxiing too fast and I said 'OK' and kept right on going. I knew what I was doing. Neil didn't fly on the way to Houston either. I flew the airplane there. All the astronauts that flew with me were: Deke Slayton, Pete Conrad, Gordon Cooper, Wally Shirra, and of course, Neil Armstrong. Ted

Mendenhall also flew with me but he never made it to the moon. These guys wanted all the information on the T-38 as they would be using this sleek little jet trainer to keep proficient in flying airplanes. We'd take off and go supersonic then turn around and come back; it was a rather interesting marketing assignment, as they were all first class pilots, and knew what to do by their test cards.

I would have to say Pete Conrad did the most risky flying of all the guys. He wanted to see a single engine capability, so we had a go around with it! I shut one engine off and pulled it back to idle to simulate engine out and then that was it. That was the best simulation; we were very low on fuel and ready to make a touch and go when we came around. So I had set up a single engine simulation by reducing the power on the one engine. That was very dangerous I realized later, because we found out that we were at less thrust than required and the T-38 had more drag than originally analyzed. Two guys had an accident in a T-38 with a single engine touch and go. We learned it was too marginal to do what we had done because of the thrust. When those two had the accident, it had less performance than anticipated. Sometime later, I saw Pete and told him about it. Also, there had been an incident of a colonel being injured in a hard landing doing the same thing with less thrust. So I guess we were just plain lucky and maybe the fact we were low on fuel was the saving grace.

ASTRONAUT CHARLES "PETE" CONRAD WITH DICK

*To Dick Thomas
Enjoyed flying with you
— best wishes
Charles Conrad jr.*

• • •

THE RENO AIR RACES

My adrenalin was just working overtime to get into my next thrill…Harold's Transcontinental Trophy Dash, Reno, Nevada. It wasn't enough that I was flying almost every day at Edwards, but I was just itching to get something else going on the side. I met a couple of guys at one of the QB (Quiet Birdmen fraternity) meetings and they were talking about putting this F4U Navy job in the Reno Air Races. Immediately my blood pressure jumped to that idea and I started thinking about flying in that race day and night. The more I thought about it the more excited I got. And before I knew it I had volunteered to fly their F4U in the race.

My announcement to Cynda did not go over exactly as I had planned. It took me away from the family even more; as I and my partners had to spend hours and hours working on the plane getting it in shape to race. We weren't exactly

A and P mechanics, but we thought we knew enough to make that plane into a darn good racer. Unfortunately for us all, we really didn't do a very thorough job and I would find that out during the race.

The Reno Air Races had always piqued my imagination, and the thought I might join their group as a participant kept me working hard on the F4U. We were short on funds and didn't really have a sponsor, but the three of us scraped up enough to get us in the race and get the airplane ready. The race was from Milwaukee to Reno. So you had to fly to Milwaukee first, and of course that first leg was weather most of the way. I ended up having to put the plane down someplace in Colorado, and fix a leaking oil line. If my memory is correct it was Grand Junction. We got that fixed and went on into Milwaukee.

On September 14, 1969, I took off from Milwaukee with fifteen other pilots. There were six F-51 Mustangs, three P-51 Mustangs, two F8F Bearcats, one MMI Mustang, one Hawker Sea Fury, one E33 Bonanza and me in the F4U Vought. There were several who never finished at all, either the weather or airplane problems. I had airplane problems all the way to Reno along with weather and finished dead last in the ones who made it to Reno. When I landed, there was quite a flurry as both stacks were hanging from the exhausts upon landing. My crew was pretty shocked I made it at all with those conditions. They said if the stacks had fallen off completely the airplane would have probably exploded in mid air. I didn't know if that was true or just BS on their part. Oh well just another learning curve.

After that expensive lesson, it was back to business as usual. I had scared myself enough on this perilous adventure. Cynda made it pretty clear to me that she wouldn't go along with another escapade like this again. And for some reason I had to agree it had been a bad idea.

Fate was about to deal me another blow that would go straight to my heart. The powers that be were putting their heads together and making a plan to surplus me. In frank words, kick my butt out. Not because of my ability, but because of my personality and disagreement with their management policies. Hank and I both disliked our immediate supervising personnel. But the VP who hired me knew nothing of their plan and even though they were 'happier' without me, the karma would turn on them eventually.

So in May of 1970, I came home from work on a Friday night and told Cynda I was without a job. She didn't react like I thought she would, but said we would make it through without the blankity-blank Northrop so-and-sos. We had saved a little more than $50,000 at this time so we weren't going to starve and I thought I could probably go to work for an airline making better money. Well, that wasn't to be because the airlines were laying-off too. There were a couple of friends that were crane operators and also flew a little. I had met them during the days of the Reno Air Races. They talked me into starting a crane company with most of the $50,000. That wasn't what Cynda had in mind though and she really wasn't happy to see me do this. But, regardless of her opinion, I had made up my mind to go into this business…to make lots of money! So in 1970, I started the Comet Crane Company. After struggling for three years to make ends meet, and sending Cynda into the aerospace work place by necessity, I was rehired by Northrop's VP, Welko Gasich in January, 1973. He was the same VP that had hired me originally, ten years earlier in 1963. I am almost positive those guys who hated me so much were biting themselves!

CHAPTER 12

REPRIEVE BY NORTHROP AND SPIN TESTS

✦

So I threw away my greasy crane clothes and tried to look professional again. Honestly looking very thin and really worn, I had been to hell and back. But a new lease on life and the idea of flying again renewed my depressed soul. I was thankful to have the job, even though Northrop would never give me back my original seven years, after laying me off without sufficient reason. They had hired another pilot to take my place during the interim. He had not been to test pilot school and had very little flight test experience. There was still an undercurrent going on in flight test which wasn't comfortable. But hopefully I had learned my lesson. And my mind was made up to make friends with those enemies. Again, I was assigned to Edwards AFB and my new boss was Hank Chouteau, the Chief Test Pilot. We saw eye-to-eye on most everything and I tried to follow his approach to dealing with engineering. The main reason I was hired back was to help Hank with the testing on the F-5E, during the next two years, 1973 through

1975. Then in 1975 I was selected by Northrop (Hank) to do the spin tests on the F-5E and the F-5F.

On a beautiful morning at Edwards Air Force Base, I took off in the brand new F-5F. It was September 25, 1975, the first flight. A small problem occurred on takeoff and it gave them all a little scare, but I was in control and flew to an altitude of about 43,000 ft. for a little over 40 minutes and completed a successful first flight. The F-5F was a new two-seat basic advanced trainer.

FIRST FLIGHT OF THE NEW NORTHROP F-5F, EDWARDS AFB

Having a first flight under my belt, I finally felt satisfied that at last I was a real test pilot. I wrote the following memo in my log that week after the first flight. Perhaps my feelings are revealed to the core from this journal.

'A real test pilot would have gone very high or very fast right? Well a lot of them have and I had always marveled at the likes of NAA's Bob Baker and Lockheed's Jim Eastham and Bill Park. Strangely enough I never have gone above 55,000 feet or faster than 1.6 MACH. I had to fly bombers to get to high altitude and dive fighters vertically to get to high MACH. Anybody who has ridden on the Concorde airliner has gone faster and higher!'

'Why am I someone a lot of people know? I have never won an air race or set a world class record; although I have taxied at least 24,000 miles going to and from the runways at hundreds of airfields. Well if Ted Turner is the 'mouth of the south', I am 'tell it like it is Thomas'. That approach gets you remembered…for all the wrong things. For example; after the first flight of the F-5F, a company vice president asked me for a statement on how it flew. My reply was technical and he wanted it political for the audience where he was conducting the interview. We conflicted. I said, "The airplane requires excessive airspeed for lift off, due to the nose wheel. It needs to be corrected before operational people start objecting."

He wanted me to talk in the normal glowing terms test pilots use in reporting the results of first flight. Surely the more tactful first flight pilots say things such as George Welch said to a general officer after the first F-86 flight, "Sir you have a very fine airplane here."

In George's case North American Aviation did have a really fine fighter. Today's 'Right Stuff' bull-------s are prone to say 'we achieved everything we planned and the airplane performed admirably'; 'We reached all of our first flight goals'; or 'Everything went as planned'. You would never hear the outrageous truth, which even I learned to cover up later on in my flying career.

Flying the F-5E and F was probably the most fun a guy could imagine. The airplane was a great performer and even though it had a few problems, working the kinks out was a hell-of-a-ride as you will find out soon!

◆   ◆   ◆

F-5E and F5F Spin Tests

While at Northrop those early years, I was quite active in the test pilot's organization called the Society of Experimental Test Pilots. A group of pilots the world over who had more hairy stories then 'Harry Potter' and told them with such gusto, you knew they had to be making them up! But, in fact, most of them were true. Anyway, my return to Northrop brought back those delicious times when we got together, drank too much, told dirty jokes, ached to achieve more and loved the camaraderie simply because they were dare-devils too. Finally, I was back in my own skin again and feeling like I had arrived as I had been selected as the company pilot to do the spin tests on the F-5E and F-5F, it was 1975.

Spin tests were not like a roller coaster in a controlled environment. Yes, they provided a thrill beyond belief, but it was the thrill of trying to control something that was out of control. If a drive in my Jag to Edwards, in the early cool desert morning, was a wake-up call…then the spin tests were the coup de grace. One had to walk that fine line between sane and crazy to do this kind of testing, quite a challenge. I was able to rise to the occasion; but initially when they told me what the program was about, I was hesitant.

When the Vice President said that I would have to literally put the plane into an uncontrollable spin and then try to recover it, I thought it was a joke. Later though, I found out from Hank Chouteau that it was no joke; and that he had been recruited to perform the spin tests of the YF-5A in 1964. His greatest spin test was a 6,000 foot free fall backwards! Wow what a ride.

We both had families and if we were killed doing these high risk programs, was Northrop going to provide for our wife and kids? Hank was in the same boat that I was but we never discussed it much…just business as usual you might say. And since no one in management seemed to act like it was a big deal, neither did we. After all, they acted like it was just standard procedure at Northrop. So we took on their same demeanor. The engineers were concerned about loosing the airplane! But pilots were expendable; after all they gave us parachutes!

The F-5E was about to give me a new status at Northrop, not that they would like me any better. No, they weren't that kind of company, but I would at least get their attention and some of the smarter ones would realize I had some talent. I have to pause and thank Hank, he did a lot for me, and I gleaned what I could from his experiences on past spin tests. However, this was 1975, and Hank, as Chief Test Pilot was totally involved in the YF-17. He had flown the first flight on this aircraft, Northrop's newest creation, in 1974. (Note: the YF-17 was in competition with the YF-16 which won the fly-off for the Air Force. However, the Navy liked the YF-17 which would later become the F-18 purchased by the Navy.)

Hank was demonstrating the new YF-17 for Northrop, and was preparing for several air shows to be performed in numerous locations all over the world.

This preparation consisted of practicing his performance several times at the Palmdale/Northrop facility. On one of those occasions, Cynda and Bettiann were invited to watch his show from the Northrop facility. They were taken to the roof of the Northrop Hanger for a bird's-eye view of his aerobatic show. As Hank took off in the YF-17 and started his air show, Bettieann began to tremble and shake watching his execution of this electrifying performance. At one point Cynda thought that 'Betts' might pass out from shaking so violently. Cynda was trying to hold her tightly so she wouldn't fall from the roof. After the show was over and Hank landed, she calmed down to normal. We all thought how funny it was that she was so traumatized by his show. Cynda would eventually have a go with this too, watching me fly the CASA C-101 at the air show in Farnborough, England.

So the spin tests on the F-5E began. The Air Force always controls the program as they are in fact the customer of the contractor building the craft, which was Northrop. The flying is like a double-edged sword in that, Northrop was responsible for the aircraft and its capabilities, but the Air Force would make the call. Consequently, Northrop pilots would be the first to fly the spin tests and give the results. And then the Air Force pilot would do approximately the same thing and decide if they agreed with the contractor pilot. It probably is useless to explain the friction that could (and often did) occur between the pilots and engineers on the opposite sides. Nevertheless, any changes that were required by the customer, (Air Force) would have to be dealt with by the contractor. Therefore, minor refinements would be made and another spin test flown, again by the contractor pilot first, followed by the Air Force pilot. The fact that Northrop was responsible for the airplane if it was lost in a spin test, gave them the right to put the pilot of their choice in the cockpit 'first'. Northrop had to make the decision to change their engineering design to meet the Air Force's requirement.

In order to make the F-5E airplane 'spin' you pull back on the stick and start going straight up. At some point the plane runs out of airspeed and quits flying, and then it actually starts sliding or falling backwards. That is when you try to recover the airplane to level flight. If the airplane fails to recover and starts to spin round and round with the nose down, you will be loosing altitude. When the predetermined altitude is reached and you have not been able to recover, you must pop the chute. This will stop the spin and hang the airplane in the sky with the nose pointed down. Sometimes you might have to restart an engine or even two to get level flight going again. The chute is jettisoned and level flight is recovered. Sounds like fun huh?

During the next few months, in fact from August, 1975, to February, 1977, we had the time of our lives with the spin tests on these airplanes. There were many incidents that would raise the hair on anyone's head. From here on I will try to recap some of the more violent or turbulent escapades that happened during the more than 107 spin tests and six hundred maneuvers that I personally performed for Northrop on the F-5E and F-5F airplanes.

It happened that a Vietnam pilot, training in the F-5E shoved the stick full forward and the aircraft departed into a negative G rolling maneuver. The pilot became disoriented and safely ejected. Surprisingly, the aircraft landed in the Arizona desert with minimal damage. The aircraft never flew again, but was used as a training device for maintenance training. However, the accident caused the Northrop Aerodynamics Engineers to look at the wind tunnel data associated with the F-5E at negative angles of attack. What they noticed was that with the flaps down and approximately six degrees angle of attack, the outer portion of the wing would stall. But, the wing leading edge would still be an effective negative lifting surface. Due to all the negative lifting surfaces, the airplane would continue in a negative G rolling condition even with pilot control stick held full aft. This tendency for the aircraft to 'tuck' into a sustained negative G flight condition (with maneuver flaps down) was termed as 'Inverted Pitch Hang-up'(IPH), since the aircraft was 'hung up' in a negataive G condition, even with stick full aft.

The F-5E was the worst case scenario. I figured out how to get it in the worst spins and a lot of people thought that it was grand. Joe Gallagher, a Vice President at the time, thought it was a daring display of fearless spirit. I had to tell what happened after it happened. I had followed procedure, and then suddenly the aircraft went nose over tail tumbling through the sky. I was thinking all the time…'hot dog' here it goes!

The 'inverted pitch hang-up' maneuver spins with the F-5E airplane were so severe the plane would literally go backwards with the nose pointed straight up.

Then the plane would fall back, nose over tail tumbling into a flat inverted spin. I couldn't even tell what I was doing. If it didn't do something wild, I was disappointed. My friend, Andy, finally said I was addicted to adrenaline. It was really something; and I needed my daily dose, a breathless ride in the sky!

It was at this point I was sent up in the F-5E to force the aircraft into the negative angle of attack region, involving negative Gs, and get the aircraft into the 'inverted pitch hang-up'. I had to let the airplane develop the negative G pitching and rolling maneuvers, that ensued from the 'inverted pitch hang-up', then I applied the control technique of 'flaps up and full aft stick'. This was the engineers' speculation that should recover the aircraft. These IPH negative G pitching and rolling maneuvers became very disorienting to me and subjected me to excessive negative Gs. This maneuver was not immediate and required several thousand feet of altitude before the aircraft became fully recovered. So the 'Thomas Recovery Maneuver' was very simple, 'flaps up, stick aft', it recovered every time. No lie! It turned out to be a famous maneuver. It was one of those days when you have an unusual 'aha'. At the time, I had to tell the engineers what I did. I couldn't tell them, because I really didn't know exactly what had happened. I know that doesn't make sense, but it is true. Eventually, we knew what I did, and this maneuver to recover is now used universally. Someone had to try it for the first time and that was me, Dick Thomas.

PICTURES OF SPIN TESTS ON F-5E

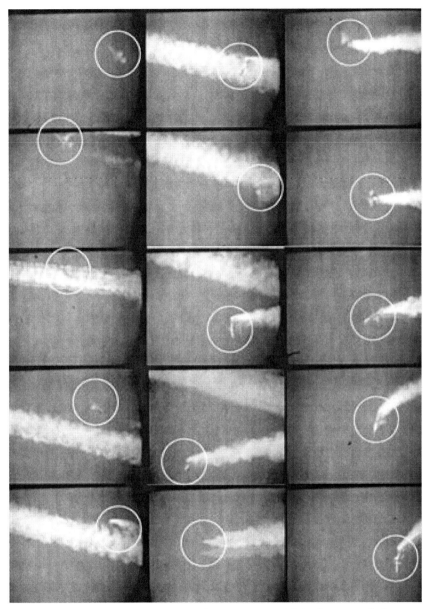

(Please note, these stills were taken from every fifth frame of the actual film to give you a small example of the tremendous tumbling that took place during the tests. Start at the top-left of the picture going down, then back to the top- middle frame and down, and the same for the last line of film. The very last frame shows a small black dot above the airplane—that is the deployed chute to stop the free falling airplane. The chute is then released from the airplane and the pilot restarts the engines and flies back to base and lands. There is a video of the actual film on the web sight of the book that you can view if you are interested. To view go to www.hellofaride-spintests.com)

Then we started doing the F-5F spin tests, we just knew it wouldn't go into a spin. The engineering data had shown it was less likely to spin than the F-5E. The F-5F was a two place trainer and had a different configuration for the wings; and the nose was another three feet longer. All the engineers and the VP who were working with us were in agreement. So as usual, I was doing exactly what I was told to do on the flight card, a 4-G turn and... *Whoops*! There it goes! If I hadn't had a recovery chute, I don't know if I could have recovered this one. Everybody was uptight, we had to go back and study this anomaly asking ourselves why it spun. The engineers were in worse of a quandary now than before, as even we pilots told them it probably wouldn't spin and it did.

We had done so many flights in the spin program and we still didn't know why the F-5F would go out of control so easily. Andy Skow, and Andy Titiriga, (both great engineers on the program), came up with the idea of a 'shark nose'. With this new configuration, it was even more unlikely that it would spin; however, the F-5F went seriously out of control on the first test. This really flabbergasted us; and took the wind out of our sails to think we had made such a mistake, since it didn't have the tendency to go into that mode according to the engineering data. It was very hard to go back to the Air Force and tell them we were wrong. So back to testing again, it turned out to go into a spin five times before recovery. In fact I put five chutes out; unrecoverable five times.

Those spin chutes are always a dicey proposition. There have been instances on more than one program where they pulled the chute and the chute came out, but it left the airplane. So pulling the spin chute is not always a guarantee. And as a matter of fact, we found out later in the program that the spin chute, although it was deploying all right, the force was so great it was blowing the O-ring that held the back plate in; and the back plate was traveling forward. If we hadn't had such close tolerances between this device and the structure, it would have blown off and away the chute would have gone.

I probably wouldn't have been around for the fourth or fifth spin test. And, if you don't recover the airplane and you have to go ask for another one, they may not give you one. Generals are funny about that. I remember General Connelly was up there and he'd say when he saw us coming to brief, "Are you guys back again? I don't want to hear anymore of this but go ahead and brief."

It was February 1977; now that the spin tests on the F-5E and F-5F were finished, what next? Northrop had just told me they were going to loan me to the Spanish Company, CASA, to assist them with developmental flying of their brand new C-101 jet trainer they were building. It would be a two-phase contract with the Northrop team setting up the actual flight test program. It was understood that CASA was, shall I say, 'very green' regarding this type of operation. This was their first jet trainer and they had some very capable talent in their engineering department, but they had some very inexperienced older pilots who didn't have a clue how to set up a flight test program.

I would be leaving sometime in May or June. Now I was quite excited about this adventure. I convinced Northrop they would need to send my wife and children to Spain during the summer. This was not unusual and Northrop agreed, then the family became rather intrigued too. I was preparing my family and trying to get things in order as I would be gone for a period of six to seven months. All of our kids were in school and would not be out of school till the middle of June. So that meant I would not see them for at least two months. Cynda wasn't working at Lockheed at that time, luckily for us all as she had been furloughed for a while. She needed to be briefed on everything, insurance, company benefits, etc. before I left.

During the Spain preparation process, Northrop decided I should give a paper in Lucerne, Switzerland, regarding the spin tests on the F-5E and F-5F. So I was given a few days to write the speech and prepare film for that presentation. Fall back and regroup, get clothes ready for the Society of Experimental Test Pilots European Symposium and Banquet. Write my speech and get films prepared along with spread sheets, charts and everything else, including a new tuxedo for the banquet. It seemed like there were never enough hours in the day to get everything done going in three different directions. I was actually finishing my speech on the airplane to Lucerne. I thought to myself, I'm going into this half-assed and sure to make a poor showing for the company. I reread my speech over and over, changing things as I went and nervously thinking does anything make sense to anyone.

I arrived and settled into my hotel. Nervous wasn't the word for it, as I felt I had been thrown a bone and literally dropped it in the quagmire. The next day the symposium started and there were many speakers as usual. It was soon to be my turn. As I approached the podium for my turn at the mike, I was a little unsure of my speech; however I knew my subject matter very well.

The Northrop film had somehow collected black fuzzy hairs from static electricity during the flight over. As I started my presentation running the film, I was appalled to see all those curly black lines on the beginning of the film. So, being the joker I am, my opening statement went something like this: "Well, we knew in the beginning that these spin tests were going to be very 'hairy' and as you can see from the film, they certainly were!"

This witty utterance brought down the house with laughter and set the stage for me to relax and give them what they wanted to hear. It was my first big presentation for the Society of Experimental Test Pilots and I felt good about it at last. As the time approached for the banquet that night, dressed in my tuxedo, I stepped into the elevator and met up with a fellow presenter. He acknowledged me and started conversation about our speeches, he was just adamant that he had won the Best Technical Paper Award. I had heard his speech and totally agreed with him that he probably had. We continued on to the banquet room together and found our table which ironically was the same. As the awards ceremony progressed, he got even cockier about his position. Finally, the announcement came and there were two people at the table that were shocked, as the winning name announced was Richard G. Thomas, Test Pilot for Northrop Corporation for his Speech "F-5E Spin Avoidance Testing". I was embarrassed for him and stunned that I had won, but the feeling of winning for me was the best reward I could have had. Even though time restrictions had been almost impossible, I proved to myself and Northrop, I could come through in a pinch. Here is my speech from that night in Lucerne, as I wrote it (but probably not as I spoke it).

F-5E SPIN AVOIDANCE TESTING
By Richard G. Thomas, Engineering Test Pilot, Northrop Corporation

The F-5E spin avoidance tests were conducted to determine if there were any undefined characteristics which would result in departures leading to a spin or unrecoverable flight conditions. By January 1975, certain operational reports indicated that an investigation of the post-stall gyrations and departure characteristics would be beneficial to the F-5E squadrons. At this time, the U.S. Air Force approved a Spin Avoidance Test Program. Spin avoidance testing is a method of evaluating the aircraft susceptibility to depart controlled flight or to enter a spin without intentionally promoting a spin. This testing is based on the directives contained in U.S. MIL specs. The primary effort in this type of testing is directed towards placing the aircraft into control forced post-stall gyrations of increasing duration and relying on the pilot's judgment to apply recovery control based on the aircraft feel in an attempt to prevent spin entry. If the aircraft actually progressed through the post-stall phase into a spin, the total envelope would be defined.

Since the aircraft was obviously going to enter out of controlled flight, we made provisions for recovery, if aerodynamic controls failed to do the job. A 24-foot ring slot parachute was installed on the tail in the area normally occupied by the landing drag chute. This installation was slightly larger than the drag chute installation because the system included a mortar for ballistic deployment with 75 feet of risers to insure adequate recovery capability. This chute system was tested at slow speed -50 kts (knots) during taxi, and in flight at 110 KIAS (Knots Indicated Air Speed) and 190 KIAS for maximum structural loads. In addition, the aft section of the fuselage was modified to take these loads and a battery operated back-up system was installed for dual engine out flight control power. Cockpit instrumentation added a sensitive accelerometer, direct reading angle-of-attack gage, sideslip angle indicator, yaw rate indicator, and spin direction indicator lights.

Pilot flight preparation was accomplished by flying two spin orientation flights in a T-33 and one flight in a U.S. Navy T-2C Buckeye. The T-2C flight was the most productive since the aircraft is basically unrestricted and will perform any positive or negative "G" maneuver including longitudinal tumbling and cart wheeling. The important benefit was exposure to extreme attitude changes and high angular rates. Since aircraft generally do not spin the same and post-stall gyrations vary, the idea of training to spin one aircraft type by flying another aircraft is basically limited to this preparation as a means of enhancing the test pilot's ability to be as relaxed as possible and thereby provide the maximum qualitative description of his visual impressions. This benefit might have been worth another flight or two-part way through the program because the tests did not produce sufficient day-to-day excursions.

For pilot flight cards we use the type of simple box presentation showing stick position and rudder application. The entry airspeed and power settings were established well in advance of starting the maneuver so control was easily monitored by the telemetry station where the engineers could verify everything with sufficient time to request verbal comment if questions arose during run-in. As shown on the card, all entry maneuvers were started at 35,000 feet and a mandatory chute deployment altitude for out-of-control maneuvers was 25,000 feet. The 25,000 foot altitude was determined based on the altitude to recover from a chute deployment plus the altitude required to glide to a landing with both engines flamed out.

The tests were conducted in the following phases in an attempt to evaluate whether the operational pilot could be expected to avoid a spin with the cues available in the uninstrumented aircraft.

Phase A: Tactical maneuvers and stalls performed with normal control inputs.

Phase B: Aborted tactical maneuvers and stalls performed with brief aggravated control inputs of less than one second duration.

Phase C: Aborted tactical maneuvers and stalls performed with sustained aggravated control inputs of up to three seconds duration.

Phase C+:   Aborted tactical maneuvers and stalls performed with grossly aggravated control inputs of up to 15 seconds but excluding deliberate spin attempts.

An aggravated control input is any control input which would tend to produce or prolong post-stall oscillations.

Erect or inverted departures were defined as uncommanded motion which developed above the stall AOA (Angle of Attack). These uncommanded motions were generally considered as a departure if they tended to diverge until recovery controls were applied. This was not completely pure because roll oscillations (wing rock) were not defined as departures.

A spin, erect or inverted, was defined as uncommanded motion above stall AOA which had a continuous yaw direction about the body axis for 360 degrees of rotation.

Maneuvers were flown so as to vary the rate of approach to stall. Smooth one "G" entries were approached using a one knot per second deceleration and smooth accelerated stalls were approached using a control rate to produce an angle of attack (AOA) rate of approximately one degree per second. The abrupt entries were performed initially using an AOA rate of approximately four degrees per second. This rate was gradually increased to the maximum attainable AOA rate of the airplane.

As external configurations were changed, a range of maneuvers were performed encompassing different energy levels in terms of airspeed/Mach number and various control misapplications. Smooth or abrupt control application in these tests defined the control rate near stall conditions.

Decelerating wind-up turns at constant altitude were performed with both smooth and abrupt entries to obtain the effect of rapidly decreasing airspeed accompanied by high forcing control inputs about all axes. Entry airspeed was varied from approximately 230 KIAS to 1.1 MACH to produce a wide range of energy levels at the entry conditions.

The tactical maneuvers performed consisted of zooms to zero airspeed, high speed yo-yo-s, aborted Immelmans and high "G" reversals. Entry airspeed was varied from approximately 230 KIAS to 1.1 MACH to produce a wide range of energy levels at the entry conditions.

The inverted maneuvers consisted of rapid push-overs from high pitch attitude, low airspeed and simple inverted stalls with full forward stick.

The investigation covered two general areas: (1) Determining the erect (positive G) characteristics for all configurations and, (2) Determining inverted (negative G) characteristics for the clean aircraft and for the centerline tank empty conditions. The erect conditions were evaluated first and they confirmed the previously recorded test data. The erect one "G" stall and the erect accelerated stall for the F-5 have similar characteristics. The stall is indicated by the onset of buffet well in advance of stall, followed by mild roll oscillations accompanied by yaw oscillations as the stall angle of attack is reached. The oscillations in roll and yaw will increase in magnitude beyond the stall angle of attack until a dynamic angular limit is reached. If full aft stick is maintained beyond the stall condition, the aircraft will develop pitch oscillations and will remain in this condition until the aft stick pressure is relaxed. The magnitude of the oscillations and rate will vary dependent on the rate of control input preceding the stall and the center of gravity. The maximum full aft stick angle of attack is 28 degrees for the one "G" stall and approximately 40 degrees for accelerated stalls. The angle of attack increase during accelerated stalls is caused by the sideslip/angle of attack coupling associated with roll-yaw oscillations which results in an increase in nose up pitching moment. During the test program it was determined that these oscillations could be forced to diverge above the stall AOA by prolonged rudder or aileron during high speed conditions.

The basic program covered eight configurations and resulted in 107 flights with 625 maneuvers. The spin boundary was defined as a result of data from 79 departures, 11 erect spins, and 6 inverted spins. The spin boundary plots correlate yaw rate and AOA. When the boundary was reached the result usually produced an oscillatory spin; if recovery controls were applied at the boundary, it would probably recover aerodynamic. When recovery controls were delayed until yaw rate and AOA were well inside of the boundary, aerodynamic recoveries did not occur.

Final U.S. Air Force/Northrop report concluded that the air combat configuration F-5E was very resistant to spins and the F-5F was resistant, but slightly less than the F-5E. This meant that both aircraft had a 'very low' probability of departing into a spin while engaged in the most aggressive maneuvering expected of the operational pilot. For centerline stored configurations a limit of 20 units (19 degrees) AOA was imposed on the aircraft.

Northrop management was not satisfied by the flying qualities and undertook steps to improve them so the operational pilots could be completely comfortable during air combat maneuvering. With these directions the engineers had to determine how to eliminate departures and spins which might occur above 40 degrees AOA.

The spin boundaries determined from actual flight test conditions were plotted from analysis of time histories of each maneuver. Further analysis concentrated first on the classic spin prediction parameter.

This analysis showed that the F-5F should be more resistant to departures and spins than the F-5E, based on the plots of AOA versus C. The actual flight test had indicated that the F-5E was slightly more resistant to departures and spins. The difference was very small but it was different. As a result of this it was felt that some other aerodynamic effect was modifying the departure/spin prediction parameter.

The basic analysis showed the F-5E weaker in dynamic directional stability near stall than the F-5F. This proved to be dihedral effect of wing fences on the F-5F which were not on the F-5E. The other obvious information from the data was the AOA reached during dynamic pitching conditions. The F-5E reached 40 degrees AOA and for similar conditions the F-5F was obtaining 50 degrees AOA. Wind tunnel and water tunnel data showed a strong nose vortex asymmetry at these high AOA's. At AOA's below 35 degrees the vortex action was weak compared to dynamic directional stability and even favorable for side-slip angles greater than zero. Since the F-5F with its longer nose would reach higher dynamic AOA's, it was exposed more often to large vortex asymmetries and departed a little more frequently.

At this point, the engineers started a Northrop funded effort to develop an aerodynamic modification which would eliminate departures in the high AOA areas (above 40 degrees). This was felt to be a more satisfactory solution than electronically limited controls or handbook restrictions. If any of you recall our spin panel discussion in Sweden last year, there was no conclusion. Some of you felt that electronic stability was acceptable and some of you felt that aerodynamics should be designed to do the job. I now feel we have a strong case of aerodynamics.

(At this point I started with a look at the classic spin prediction parameter film and slides.)

In the lower AOA (below 35 degrees) it predicted the F-5E would be more likely to depart than the F-5F because of the reduced cn near stall. The flight test results show the F-5F to be slightly more likely to depart. The difference appeared to relate to the dynamic AOA reached during maneuvers. The F-5E obtained approximately 40 degrees AOA and the F-5F peaked at approximately 50 degrees AOA during dynamic conditions. In these high AOA's static directional stability if near zero and the pilots confirmed this with reports of no rudder power at high AOA. The dihedral effect was still positive so the engineers felt they had an aerodynamic effect related to the leading edge extension (LEX) and the nose shape. A water tunnel and wind tunnel investigation was started to determine the nose vortex patterns on the production nose shape. These tests showed that the nose was generating asymmetric vortices. Below 35 degrees AOA these asymmetries were developing yawing moments which were stabilizing for sideslip angles greater than zero. Above 35 degrees AOA the asymmetries were causing a stronger yawing moment which was unstable.

Tunnel tests were started to develop an aerodynamic change which would control these asymmetric vortices. It was found that stakes on the radome held the vortices very symmetrical through the higher AOA's. This also eliminated the stable yawing moments at sideslip angles greater than zero. Modifications were continued until the 'shark nose' evolved. This particular shape retained the favorable yawing moments due asymmetric vortices at the lower AOA and held the symmetric vortex formation at the higher AOA in the water tunnel and wind tunnel tests.

As a pilot it was hard to believe this kind of magic. At the same time we determined that a change to the leading edge extension (LEX) in the forward wing root area would be favorable to increasing dynamic directional stability in the stall AOA region. This modification would also increase the 1 "G" trimmed AOA.

Next we obtained U.S. Air Force approval to fly another series of flights with Northrop funding. This testing was limited to three configurations and maneuvers were selected from the most adverse conditions of the basic program. As a result, we moved toward conditions which departed or spun the F-5E and the F-5F after some baseline stall data was obtained. This was accomplished on the F-5F aircraft since it was still configured for spin testing. The results were an aerodynamicist's dream and it even impressed fellow pilots. (See CD of Spin film)

From these tests it was concluded that the air combat configured aircraft (both F-5E and F-5F) could be unrestricted and the centerline stored configuration limits could be raised to an AOA limit of 29 units (32 degrees) when equipped with the shark nose and LEX!

◆   ◆   ◆

THE ACCIDENTAL SPIN

In 1980 I was called back to Edwards AFB, from my 'black world' job to do the spin tests for high angle of attack on the Saudi Arabian F-5F. This particular version of the F-5F had a refueling probe running along one side of the plane. Because of this probe, the Saudi pilots were having problems with the stability. Northrop had set limits on the spin tests we were to do for the Saudis, and I was the first to fly the test. Even though we had prepared the airplane with an emergency chute, we were not going to go beyond the valley of departure or in other words spin the airplane. Well, it didn't quite work out that way as I recall. And I will call this the 'accidental spin'. As I prepared to put the airplane to the point on the flight test card; I steadied my elbow on my knee. All of a sudden my elbow slipped off my knee and I am in a flat spin. There was no way I could recover the airplane and I was forced to use the chute. The truth of this was I shouldn't have been flying in this 'pissed off' state of mind, but to put it bluntly those few Northrop people put the screws to me and hung me out to dry. Luckily for me there was someone 'up there' watching over me.

Captain Roy Martin was the Air Force pilot that flew this program with me. We became flying comrades and he eventually resigned from the Air Force to become a Northrop Test Pilot. Cynda and I went to Chouteau's that night for a steak dinner. I hadn't said a word to her about what happened and the minute we walked in, Bettiann, shouted out. "Dick wasn't supposed to spin the airplane and he did."

Cynda didn't know what to think and looked rather blank at the time. Later, she got a pared down version of the story from me and it was not as bad as Betts had made her think. The truth would come out sooner or later; and as this book will reveal, it is about twenty-eight years later that their ruthless treatment of me is about to be told.

Oh well just another day at the office, business as usual. Just another 'simple test' as some engineers would call it. There were always Air Force test pilots involved with the spin tests and sometimes we became friends, and sometimes life was difficult. At this juncture, I would like to personally comment about this Air Force pilot who would become a close personal friend. Roy Martin was my junior by about fifteen years or more. His philosophy ran quite serious to business, and our thinking seemed to agree on most spin test issues. Another aha was he had graduated from Parks Aeronautical College of St. Louis University, my own alma mater. Let's just say Roy and I were two guys who thought along the same lines when it came to flying.

When that spin test was finished a party was planned at the Thomas house, all those involved were invited whether it was Air Force or Northrop. It wasn't so much a celebration, but rather a party of relief that I hadn't killed myself from frustration. Our home was full of people from the lowest ranking person on the totem pole on up from Edwards. Roy and I were the 'stars' of course, and it was one of those happy times when lots of drinking and joking was going on. Underneath it all, I was seething about the whole fiasco. I knew what was going on from those slithering idiots in charge in Hawthorn (who were not invited). But, thank God, I was out of here the following week and back to the 'black world' where I was actually respected for having a brain and using it well.

Unbeknownst to me, Roy had written a poem about me. So before the evening began to slack off, he stood on our balcony dining room floor called attention to everyone and here is the poem he read:

THE SAGA OF SLICK DICK THE SUPERSONIC STICK

Slick Dick, as he's known around this place,
With a three-piece suit and cigar in his face.
But it's not the man, for which this story is told,
This saga is about his hands of gold.
For, you see when he grabs a hold of the stick,
Shock waves would form from the hands of Slick Dick.
When he flew, you never knew if he was coming back,
For his specialty was the hazardous high angle of attack!
His weather reports were the best we've seen,
But lookout if it's cloudy in the San Joaquin.
He would pull on that pole and stomp on that rudder,
"And there she goes" is all he would utter.
Full forward stick and aileron with,
Any thoughts of recovery were only a myth.
The yaw rate was high the alpha was up,
Occasionally from Dick you would here a "yup, yup".
With a "phooey", and a "shucks", and a "yep", and a "nope",
For lower angle of attack there just was no hope.
At 25 thou and still going around,
The idea now was don't hit the ground.
Out comes the chute with a pull of the lever,
I'll tell you the deployment mechanism is clever.
This time she recovers nose down with a tuck,
All we hear from Slick Dick is a relieved "ah fu--".
If you happen to visit Eddy Air Force Base,
With sonic booms happening all over the place.
It may be a Talon or a sleek Tiger II
Up there playing around in the blue.
Or maybe the reindeer and sleigh of St Nick,
Or maybe the sonic hands of Slick Dick.
Author, Roy Martin, Test Pilot-Northrop Corp.

Well, this poem really says it all; these hectic years of spin tests gave our Northrop party friends a vivid memory to take home. I guess I gave those guys hours of thrilling tail telling and laughter. But, most of all, like I said before, it was a hell of a ride and I'd do it again. The truth of this last spin will come to light eventually, as you will discover the folly of the Northrop engineering hierarchy's decisions which eventually killed not one but two pilots.

CHAPTER 13

SPAIN – 1977 & 1978

✦

In 1977, Northrop fulfilled their contract and sent me to Spain for a Spanish company, called CASA. I was to assist the Spanish Air Force with developmental flying of their new C-101 jet. It was Spain's first jet trainer that they had designed and built. This program would last during two segments, the first for almost six months in1977 and the second for four months in1978.

Since traveling to South America with Beech Aircraft in the late 50's, I had felt a real kinship with the Spanish culture; and I became enamored with the idea of going to Spain. It was my habit to indoctrinate myself with the knowledge of customs, family values and social activities of the area where my trip was taking me. I would try to fit into their life style and 'do what they did' to the best of my ability. It seemed to work on most occasions.

Thinking back, I thrived on adventure, and just the word *Spain* gave me visions of fine ladies, bull fights and a whole new world of adventure. It felt like playing the best game in the world and getting paid for it! Northrop had a vested interest in this company called CASA, and the company was about to bring in their first jet trainer. Because they were inexperienced in the technical aspects of testing, they called on Northrop to furnish a full team of engineers and an engineering test pilot to complete the structural, stability and control tests on their first airplanes. I was the lucky pilot selected to do the job. As the saying goes…"It's a dirty job, but somebody's got to do it."

During the negotiations for this contract, I realized that I would be away from the family for several months without a return trip to the states. As Cynda became informed about this, we felt she had a rather serious challenge ahead of her that summer. And I might add what it was…three teenagers ages fourteen, sixteen and eighteen. Together we decided that during the summer months, the family should visit Spain and live with me in an apartment that would be furnished by Northrop Corporation. So after school was out and arrangements made, Cynda and the kids, Heather, Rich and Velvet all flew to Madrid, in July, 1977, for a six week stay.

I had a very small Spanish Seat (car) furnished by the company. It would barely hold the five of us. The apartment I chose was inconveniently located outside of Madrid in a new complex called Las Rosas. It seemed the harder I tried to please Cynda, the worse things turned out. I truly didn't understand the workings of the complex and since it was new, the management was not in place, so consequently there was no one to complain to if things did not work properly.

Yes, you guessed it; the building elevator never worked and hadn't worked. Our apartment was on the fourth floor, we had a very small refrigerator as most Spanish women go to the bakery (panaderia) every morning to get fresh bread and to the small store for fresh milk. Although the super market was only a couple blocks away, the village was slightly hilly and the walk to the store was mostly uphill. A few days of this fourth floor apartment and walking up hill to the market seemed to wear thin on all the family and soon, I knew I had blown it again. There was a swimming pool which I thought the kids would enjoy, but the water was so cold they wouldn't get in it. There was no transportation for them because I had to have the car to get to work which left them stuck in this fourth floor apartment all day, with no TV or any entertainment. I immediately tried to get them to start using the bus from Madrid, but that didn't seem to work either.

Cynda had the worst jet lag for the first week. She couldn't wake up during the day and couldn't sleep at night. At home, we had a king size bed and the only thing furnished in the apartment was a very poor double bed with the old style mattress and open wire springs. Finally, we all began to find a way to make do with the conditions. We found we could shop at the market when I got home in the evening and everyone carried a sack of groceries up the stairs to the fourth floor. A lot of complaining and laughing went on, but we were engaged to eat out with our new Spanish friends almost every night.

We all enjoyed the social scene of Madrid, meeting each night with some of my new acquaintances from work. There were a couple of American wives married to Spanish engineers and most of the Spaniards I worked with spoke fairly good English. The Spanish are very very social and they included our teenagers in everything. My family was treated as special guests and they loved every minute of their six week stay. It was great to have them waiting for me each night. And I was grateful to Northrop for covering the expense.

Well, I had arrived earlier at CASA with great expectation. Frustration is the best word I can use in this case as nothing was as I expected it to be. It seemed that time tables meant nothing to the Spanish, it was a ho-hum attitude. They were so laid back, one who was serious about business had to wonder how they even got the airplane together. It was now June 2, 1977; so far we had been here two weeks finding apartments, checking out rental cars and doing the entire little details one must take care of in a foreign country. The word at the Air Ministry was that the CASA C-101 aircraft would make its first flight on the following Friday. This was total news to the Northrop Team as we were supposed to be in charge but knew nothing of this plan. At this point no engine runs, or taxi tests, or anything serious had been done.

During these first few weeks at CASA, the Flight Test group held meetings regarding all phases of the program. This crusty old pilot, Colonel de la Cruz, never seemed to arrive at the plant until the meetings were almost over. He was certainly a seasoned pilot, but as for getting his methodology arranged for a flight test program, he was failing miserably. It was during these first few days as we were preparing for the first flight, the Northrop team realized what we were up against, as far as Col. de la Cruz was concerned. We would travel around the plant in the company vehicle and sometimes we saw the most unbelievable things going on, it would throw us into hysterics. For instance a very funny thing happened one day as we saw de la Cruz checking his 'g' suit connection when we drove by the C-101 airplane at 3:30 p.m. on the day he thought he was going to make the first flight. It was ridiculous for a man who is 'not' to exceed two "Gs" during the first flight. He did not fly that day as the plane was not ready. Finally, I was able to run engines at 6:00 p.m. that night!

The next day the Colonel and CASA engineer Teja, had an argument which lasted thirty minutes about flight schedules. This was the first time the Northrop team had seen de la Cruz in action. The confrontation started when de la Cruz was telling them he was mad because they began the meetings in the morning when he is not available and they should know better. After the argument, de la Cruz agreed to arrive on time in the mornings. This was the picture that was presented to the Northrop team; and we knew we really had our work cut out for us, to accomplish what we had been sent here to do.

To make matters more difficult, the only handbook for the airplane was in Spanish, which was very difficult for our team, and furthermore, it would not be translated. Most of our team did not speak Spanish including me. It became increasingly difficult for the Spaniards to understand our approach. Their work ethic was so hap-hazard that the airplane structure was not even 'clean'.

Twenty days later, we were ready for taxi tests. My taxi test was first, and then Col. de la Cruz did two. He skidded the tires three times for 25 feet each time on his first taxi out. It appeared the anti-skid system was not operating properly. At the end of the run both tires went flat when the aircraft was parked. During his second high speed taxi the nose wheel was raised twice and on the second time, both tires were smoked again with the nose gear in the air. Other than that the three taxi tests went well. As I referred back to my notes, I had a lot of squawks for a taxi test!

We were finally preparing for the first flight, it was June 24, 1977, we hung around Getaffe (the Air Base near CASA) until very late waiting for information from INTA (like U.S. NASA) clearance. We finally got a note from one of their pilots that there would be no flight until Monday. On the following Saturday, June 25th, I was thankfully able to move into an apartment from my hotel, and it sure felt good. My family would be arriving soon and I was ready for them in this nice new apartment in Las Rosas.

I had received a call to go to Getafe that we might fly, it turned out to be, standby and wait. Then after midnight closer to around 1:00 a.m., I got a call from Walt Fellers, Northrop V.P., telling me we might fly Sunday. He had received a call from Teja about midnight. This kind of thing was typical of the way their operation was run. Nobody knew who was running the 'show'. To the Spanish, 1 a.m. is nothing. They never go to bed until 2 a.m. or so!

Well on Sunday morning the 26th, it was the same performance over again. We arrived to find de la Cruz calling everybody and getting nowhere with clearance. This was another false alarm and that afternoon the whole thing was called off; so we went home.

On Monday, the 27th, again it started in the typical manner with the players arriving about 10 a.m. and de la Cruz coming in about 11 a.m. No time schedule for the first flight. Then about 1:30 or 2:00 p.m. the chase airplanes from Getafe Air Base arrived unannounced to chase the flight. It was then decided that we would go to lunch. Brilliant, now it is about 3:00 p.m. and everyone who wanted lunch has eaten! Are we ready to fly? Well not really, we first have a preflight briefing scheduled. This lasts about one and a half hours, but it did not look good at this point because the sky was now very dark with thunderstorms. About 6:00 p.m. some holes begin to open and by 7:00 p.m. de la Cruz decides to fly. I am allowed to ride in the back of the only two-place airplane for chase. At this point CASA has not thought of pictures. So I find some film and take my camera. The flight finally gets off the ground and is accomplished as briefed. We leave with a second flight scheduled for sometime Tuesday. The Spanish were adamant that their pilots would fly the first and second flights in the airplane. I had no problem with that but we really couldn't get a feel for the performance as they had no knowledge of what we were really looking for.

Tuesday, the 28th, became a complete repeat of Monday, late arrival, lunch, and briefing. Again, the sky is dark with thunderstorms. The pilot, (I think it was Verano) finally gets off about 7:00 p.m., to do gear retraction. It was obvious he had not thought much about it and was totally unprepared for the warning light activating due to drop of hydraulic pressure or for the gear warning horn. The ground engineers were not prepared either and as soon as lights started flashing and horns started sounding, they told him to return immediately and land. *The debrief was strictly comic opera!* I finally left at 8:45 p.m. and laughed all the way home. The whole Northrop team was in total frustration at this point.

Wednesday, the 29th, was another absolutely hysterical day. The King of Spain, Juan Carlos, flew his own helicopter in to watch the performance. He, along with the press, were expecting to witness an 'air show' if you could call it that. Mind you, this was the third flight and they were going to give the King a show??? Things were surprisingly on schedule, but not well planned. Nobody appeared to be in charge or authorized to do anything. It was obvious that everybody wanted to be in the so-called picture. The flight got off and de la Cruz completed a small test card. Meanwhile the rest of the group kept the King standing by the runway for 30 minutes. There was no loud speaker so His Highness had no idea what was going on during the flight. He left immediately after the flight.

The absurdity of this picture had me so disgusted, I walked to the cafeteria where the Northrop people were authorized to eat and found I was invited to *a lunch time cocktail party!* Can you believe that? Then at the party of the ridiculous, I am told I 'may' fly the aircraft that afternoon, but the weather was too bad to get the data we needed. During the course of the cocktail party, I suggested we wait at least an hour, but somebody had already canceled the flight. I found this out only when I saw the chase planes taxi out to go back to Getafe. Oh well, that was the way they did things. On a happier note, I had dinner with Captain Antonio Rojas that night; he was a 'player' on the political scene I later learned.

On Thursday, the 30th, as I arrived at the CASA office in downtown Madrid. I found out there was a rumor that de la Cruz was going to fly again that day to test the speed brake trim changes. This proved to be wrong, but could easily have been true. This was the last straw, you might say, as Walt Fellers our V.P. in charge, had taken all he could and blew his stack at their Chief Engineer Puentes. Unfortunately this Spanish engineer would do nothing. Interestingly enough though, I had just happened to go by the office again and found that de la Cruz was debriefing his flight of June 29th without the Northrop team being advised. As I listened, I found there had been changes made to the aileron system without either pilot being told. We then found out that Cesar Puentes, the Spanish engineer, did a lot of stuff 'off the cuff' without briefing the necessary people and would let a pilot go out and fly cold and just try to figure it out as he went along! This was plain insanity…an accident just waiting to happen.

On July 1st, I spent the entire day writing. One thing I wrote was a memo to Gonzales, (CASA's President & CEO) which said we must have some control over these engineering changes before someone gets killed. I never was more serious about anything; somehow we needed to get their attention.

It was a continuing saga of poor discipline and worse management. The good thing was the weekends were full of unexpected activities, like bull fights, sight-seeing and just plain socializing. Old friends were there that I had known since my Boeing days. Bob Baker, who had been the North American Chief Test Pilot, was now representing the Garrett Engine Company out of Phoenix. He had checked me out in the F-100 at Edwards AFB back in 1958. He was assigned to the engine group for the C-101. And, he was currently involved with a Spanish woman named Carmen. They all were waiting anxiously to meet Cynda as I was the first American Test Pilot the Spanish had met that was not divorced!

I finally flew the 'real' first flight and all subsequent flights regarding the flight test program. During these next few weeks, there were many problems that needed attention and Don Murray and I were trying to figure out why some glitches were happening. There was a problem with the aileron centering okay at 200 KIAS (knots indicated air speed) and not centering at 120 KIAS. This related to the information that was found after my third flight. It seemed as though no one paid much attention to this sort of thing. I was so exasperated with ongoing problems; I sat down that night and wrote a letter to Hank Chouteau back home. I was hoping he could shed some light on these unanswered questions.

THE REAL 'FIRST' FLIGHT OF THE C-101 BY DICK THOMAS

The philosophy of some of the top Spanish engineers was, if there wasn't a plan; just plan it as you go along. That in itself means trouble, but they simply didn't know what to do.

The people of Spain stay out all night, eat dinner about 11:00 p.m. finally go to bed around 1:00 a.m. or later, get up about 8:00 a.m. straggle into work between 9:00 or 10:00 a.m. Do a couple hours work; go to lunch for two-hours. Drink a couple glasses of wine and mosey back to work, sometimes get serious between 4:00 p.m. and 7:00 p.m. It is very different from the work style of the United States and requires a little getting used to. The truth is Spanish people have a totally different approach to life. They really know how to live while they work, and live they do. It may be different now in these later years, but in the 1970's, it was totally safe to be on the streets at midnight with your wife and three teenagers. In fact, everyone who could walk and breathe, including babies, was socializing on the streets.

The Northrop team tried to do their work mostly in the mornings as the siesta in Spain was very much a part of the Spanish lifestyle. We even took on the two-hour lunch as common place, along with a usual glass or two of wine. Now I didn't object to a couple glasses of wine at lunch, however, there was one time when that wasn't such a bright idea. During one of those days when we leisurely discussed objectives on their new CASA C-101, an idea from one of our engineers was tossed around as to why the airplane was doing a certain thing. There were several ideas speculated at the time. As the afternoon progressed and we returned to work, I was asked to put the airplane through some of those perimeters we had discussed at lunch. After the initial shock and feeling a little guilty and maybe just a little nervous, I did go up and fly. I will say after that day's flight I would not drink wine at lunch again, if there was any chance of flying that afternoon. That was one flight I did not enjoy.

Working a few hours in the late morning till noon, then from after siesta time to early evening was about the easiest job flying I had ever enjoyed. This left plenty of time for me to enjoy the wife and kids and take them on outings every evening. After napping in the afternoon, they were ready and waiting for me when I got to the flat. The Spaniards all go out in the evening to mingle; they have their tapas and drinks and visit with their neighbors and friends. It is the most hospitable atmosphere one would ever encounter. We basically kept the same hours, getting home late each night between midnight and 1:00 a.m. There never seemed to be any crime, of course Spain had just been through a tough ruler who believed an 'eye for an eye' and would literally cut off your hand for stealing. Sometimes, I think that might be what the U.S. needs to do.

Nevertheless, the kids were given the grandest lesson of social graces they would probably ever get in a foreign country. At first they were more or less shy but eventually, they rallied to enjoy the sightseeing and historical places. But, they never stopped talking about eating the roasted baby pigs brought out on huge platters at Botin's restaurant in Madrid; or getting very large teary eyes when a baby leg of lamb with the tiny hoof still attached was served to one of our Spanish friends. Botin's was the original café in Madrid, where Ernest Hemingway hung out during his bull fight years in Spain. This was cultural education at its best. We loved the Spanish people and their carefree ways and they seemed to love us back.

I was really charmed by the experience of the bull fights. And before the family arrived, I had made friends with some of the engineers who were also enthralled with bull fighting. As I got into the Sunday habit of bull fights, I began reading and studying the history of this ostentatious ritual. It was exciting for me to watch those toreadors challenging a 1000 pound monster charging them with only a cape for protection. However, when Cynda got there, it was too exciting to her and the kids. They were more concerned with the picadors and their horses being gored. Even though the horses were heavily padded with quilted blankets, it did happen occasionally. We finally came to an agreement about this problem and started a grand tour on weekends and holidays seeing Spain.

Driving in Spain was an adventure in itself. Taxis and cars furiously going here and there honking their horns and the drivers giving you every kind of arm, hand and finger motion you could imagine. I learned that in order to get anywhere in Spain, you must be an aggressive driver. Luckily, I was able to survive the test and get where I needed to go in a reasonable time. When Cynda and the kids arrived, I had already moved to the new development, the Las Rosas area outside of Madrid about five miles. I began to get familiar with driving speeds, crazy go-a-rounds and other quirky rules regarding traffic. Fortunately for me, my family trusted my driving, but Cynda decided she absolutely could not drive in Madrid. So they were marooned on their own little island, four stories up, till old Dad got home in the evening.

During the next six weeks, we saw every imaginable sight we could possible get to see. We had many Spanish friends; their hospitality and advice were wonderful in helping us see the most important places in Spain. Our first trip included the wonderful castle in Segovia called the Alcazar. It looked like something of a fairytale castle with many conical spires. To tour the castle you entered over a heavy wooden bridge that could be drawn up with huge chains. This was the bridge over what had been a deep and expansive moat; of course there was no water in it at this juncture. This castle had been originally built in the 1072-1109 period of Spain and later added to in 1333. This was the first of many of our wonderful experiences in making life in those ancient years become a reality. Our family would get a grand lesson and historical adventure from these next few weeks of touring all over Spain.

We were so fortunate to get those weekends free to travel, and during the month of August, the whole of Spain literally goes on vacation so naturally the Northrop team had to slow the process considerably leaving me more time for the family. It would fill a book to tell you all the wonderful times we had visiting places like El Escorial, the monastery, guided by our friends, Pam and Benito de la Puerta. He had gone to school there. His wife Pam was originally from California and had gone to Spain to study at the college in Madrid. This wonderful structure of historical architecture had ancient bibles and artifacts from the earliest times, and meant so much more when native Spaniards who have lived and breathed the culture explained the purpose and value of such a place.

For example we were invited to Burgos, with our friends Barbara and Ricardo Dorado. He was born there in Burgos; his father was a famous musician and had written the Spanish National Anthem years before. Barbara was from Houston, Texas, and again came to Madrid to study. Ricardo was quick to show us the old castle ruins which stood on the hill overlooking Burgos, and told stories about the many secret underground tunnels that were dug from the castle down to the river. These were for people to escape to the river and get away safely in canoes hidden in thrushes along the banks if the castle came under siege.

Ricardo and Benito were talented engineers on the CASA C-101. Both were greatly admired by the Northrop team and very interesting to be around. Since their wives were from the United States, Cynda could get information from them about the things she was most interested in seeing, and have the pleasure of visiting with someone who spoke English during dinner.

Carmen Bazo was Bob Baker's Spanish girl friend; Cynda and she were very quick to hit it off. Now Carmen only spoke a few words of English and Cynda had studied Spanish for one year in high school; and her Spanish left something to be desired. Amazingly they were able to communicate very well, and Carmen showed Cynda the quaint shops and best areas for shopping all over Madrid. This included dealing with Spanish Gypsies who sometimes became bothersome begging for handouts, if you looked prosperous.

One of the most interesting points of history in Madrid was the Prado Art Museum. Cynda and the kids must have made that tour at least three times. It takes days to see all the different artists work and the kids may have become a little bored with it, but Cynda was in her element.

During early August, the vacation season, it was decided that I would take the family to La Monga on the Mediterranean. Driving that little 4 cylinder Seat all the way to La Monga proved rather challenging. Roads were only two lane and we had no air conditioning. The best speed I could get out of this little 'go-cart' was 55 mph, and that was floor boarded!

Sightseeing pleasure outweighed our complaining though, since our kids had seen the "Man of La Mancha" in live theatre in Los Angeles prior to visiting Spain. They were surprised when we started telling them we were actually going into the country of Don Quixote. The countryside was breathtaking; there were green rolling hills dotted with many picturesque windmills of La Mancha. As we became more involved in watching for those antique windmills, we soon forgot how warm and uncomfortable we felt.

This was our first excursion without native Spaniards leading the way; and I was quite unprepared for the trip as I didn't really understand traveling through Spain. There were no restaurants, no pit stops, and very few places to fill the car with petrol. Since we had a long six hour drive from Madrid, we needed to eat and we finally found a very unique place. It was a café of sorts, in a house. Now the cows and animals were under the house as it was built on a slight hill and appeared as a two story dwelling. Actually the animal shelter or 'barn' was like an open garage under the main floor of the house, only with dirt floors. The 'so-called café was on the top floor in the main room of the house. Ordering became an even more difficult ordeal as everything was hand-written in Spanish and we couldn't figure out what it was. I can't remember what we ate, but there was a lot of grumbling about the food. As for me, I could and did eat just about anything the Spanish served, even those pickled purple baby eels!

La Monga was a small city on the peninsula which jutted out into the Mediterranean at the southern tip of Spain. I had understood that there was a train coming back from La Monga to Madrid three days later. So I deposited the family in a nice hotel room which was walking distance to the beach and stayed one night then left the next morning to go back to Madrid. None of the Northrop group was on vacation at the time. We were there to do a job and try-ing hard to get it done.

During their stay, the kids all learned to wind surf; they were all good swimmers. Cynda was not a good swimmer and planted herself on the beach. Somehow a grain of sand scratched her eyeball and a great infection set in on the second day there. She became very ill from the infected eye, almost to the point of needing a doctor. It wasn't a great vacation for her but finally the day arrived to come home and she proceeded to find out about the train. Unfortunately, there was no train to Madrid, and her money was running out. Her next move was to contact our friend, Pam de la Puerta, in Madrid, and have her get in touch with me to purchase airline tickets on the charge card so they could get back to Madrid. I have to admit, when she let me do the planning for them, I screwed things up. In all reality, I was told there was a tram going around the peninsula for a sightseeing tour; and not a train going back to Madrid. I think Cynda was learning just how much she could count on me to arrange things, and from that point on she made decisions for the family. There were always invitations from several couples to keep us going every night of the week and almost every weekend another exciting excursion. I needed to concentrate on my job and let her do the planning.

Truth being I had enough difficulties with the language at work. Not being able to speak their language at all was a real challenge. My problem was I had to deal with the tower on every test flight. They spoke Spanish and I spoke English. There were times when I would call the tower and speak in English and it was hard to tell what you might get asked to do. My call sign was 'uno cero uno' that's one zero one. If I spoke it in Spanish, they would come back with landing instructions in Spanish. One day I tried to get across to them to speak in English. After all, they spoke English to the German pilots who came in flying the F-104s, and the German pilots spoke English hardly at all, but the two of them got along fine. Anyway, after explaining this to them, they came back again with "Si, uno cero uno!"

They gave me privileges and priorities. If I called in they would pretty well clear the pattern because mistakes in communication could happen. For instance, one day the Chief of the Spanish Air Force decided to come out and see the airplane; but he came unannounced. We didn't know when I took off that he was coming. So I'm through with the test and returning to CASA when I get this call from the Spanish flight test group and they asked, "Oh, when you come back, the Chief of the Spanish Air Force is here, would you put on a show?"

Great, I hadn't been doing show work in the airplane at all. Usually, air shows are practiced over and over to make sure you don't kill yourself. I thought what in the world can I do to demonstrate this airplane and put on any kind of a show?

As I started back, I began experimenting doing rolls from high altitude working down in altitude. I found out to do a really good low altitude roll; you had to be very careful to push forward with the stick as you rolled upside down, in order to hold the nose up as you went around. If you didn't you'd come out looking at the ground and very likely stick your nose there also.

So I practiced that all the way up this river to the field and called the tower and told them, "I'm coming in."

Of course I had priority because the Chief was on the field and he wanted to see the airplane perform. I was really stumped for what to do for his show so I only did the one thing. I came in across the field and did a slow roll about 75 ft off the ground. And, then I pulled up and came back by the tower, which was three or four stories high, and did another low roll. By this time I'm sure my pupils were dilated, my pants weren't wet yet but they should have been. As I pulled up that time, I thought, 'wow', I made it! I decided immediately, I'll not do that anymore. That was the greenest grass I had ever seen from an inverted airplane.

Well the Chief thought I was a Spanish pilot in the airplane. Nobody bothered to tell him any different, so he turned to his assistant and said "It looks very good, I'm glad we have an airplane that looks and flies like an American airplane."

I came around and landed; and when I taxied in and climbed out of the cockpit, the Chief General started talking to me in Spanish. He thought the show was really great. But I don't speak Spanish, and one of the Spanish pilots jumped in and started talking to him. Being rescued, I quickly ran into the hangar to the bathroom.

That night as I sat there alone in my apartment thinking about the day, I wrote down these reflections: *If ever a shadow of anxiety has crossed my mind where pure unmitigated terror stared me in the face, it was today! After a momentary flash of recognition, I stared back as relaxed as I had never felt before in this business. For a moment I questioned my judgment, and then with the supreme confidence which can only come from a well rehearsed mental confidence; I pressed on. Actually what amazed me was I never faltered.*

Many writers describe the 'sweat in the palms' feeling, in this business your decisions are so sudden sweat has no chance to form. It is perhaps the aftermath for an unprepared fool. I had no moments of the unprepared and I knew if I had started right the only twitch would be my involuntary reaction to the unfamiliar scene of the earth upside down. Knowing that I had started right with the right conditions gave me the confidence to press on even though the runway was pushed unfamiliarly near my canopy. That small twitch nearly cost me my life. For had I attempted to do other than what I was committed to accomplish, I would have laid 9000 pounds of jet airplane hard on the ground at a spectacular 360 Knots airspeed. This certainly would have ruined my whole day!

Therein lays a solid truth for to continue when the numbers are wrong is to willfully venture into some dark and unexplored area. In this business you must be well prepared mentally when you intend to penetrate the unknown. Those of us who have done so have frequently not lived to regret the action; for on occasion every pilot has to one degree or another been there.

I imagine that the involvement in action of others and learning from those actions, plus a small indiscretion on their own part adds up to what is called experience…

There were many facets of this airplane that were good, but the thing that worried me the most was the quality of workmanship. When I would do any kind of roll or movement, there was rattling in the airplane from different areas, you could hear nuts and bolts rolling around or pieces of trash falling from one place to another. FOD or foreign objects could and did kill pilots. We would have to address this issue sometime soon, because it worried me to no end. Again, their respect for quality was very relaxed at this time.

The Northrop team was finally making a little progress at their objective, but whether it would last after we left was another question. This was 1977 and we were just in the initial program of clearing the eighty-percent envelope. The wife and kids had gone back home to the states at the end of August, school would be starting soon. It would be several weeks or maybe months before we got together again.

I returned to my habit of attending bull fights, Sundays or weekends were very lonely after my family left. My first job was to get back into Madrid where most of my Spanish friends lived. I no longer needed a three bedroom flat, so I found a one bedroom apartment in a nice three storied place. It was easier to get places riding the subway; and close to some of my favorite night spots with my acquaintances and Northrop people. Finally, we finished the contract for the first phase and went home. We were primed to return in 1978 for the final test…the *spin tests*.

During those next few months in the states, I was sent here and there with the marketing team to demonstrate the capabilities of the F-5. I have to say traveling with George Sterling was the best; we would usually finish our day of air shows with a drink at the Officer's Club. George used to tell this story on me. It seems we were having martinis at the Canadian Air Base near Cold Lake, Canada, as the story goes, and I had my martini glass in my right hand with my thumb tucked into my belt loop. George figured I had something up my sleeve for this, but he still asked why I had my thumb in my belt loop. When I answered that I couldn't afford to spill a drop of my martini, they all just laughed. There was lots of time for jokes and buffoonery during those sales expeditions. However, I knew the time to return to Spain was shortly forthcoming.

On April 7, 1978, I found myself back in Madrid, Spain. After having been there two weeks, I realized it was true that familiarity brought comfort and relaxation. As I reviewed the situation that existed at CASA, I made up my mind I would carefully take a definite position because it appeared that they had accomplished nothing of importance since the Northrop Team left in late October, 1977.

There was a party at the Rojas' high rise flat on Friday night. There I was able to express my point of concern to Murga, the Chief Engineer, regarding their capability to perform the other 20% of the test package. They had the intelligence but simply could not coordinate the package. I was there to do the spin tests and fly in the Farnborough Airshow only, and they had not completed the initial stability and control program that included the flutter tests.

It was spring in Madrid, a warm sunny day. Reflection is a pause that refreshes, so on that gorgeous Sunday as I sat at a near-by sidewalk café drinking my favorite Spanish beer and eating a 'jamon y queso bogadea' (ham and cheese sandwich); I knew I had some unanswered questions regarding just what would be required of me.

There were some important issues hanging unsolved, like the question of the contract. I was told that Gonzales, the President of CASA, had asked for me to do the Spin Tests and fly the show for Farnborough only. But now they were telling me that they wanted an Experimental Test Pilot for participation in *all* flying. Then I was told by Alvira, the Vice President that everything was included in the contract and I was to do all the flutter testing as well. If the right hand knew what the left hand was doing, they would all be on the same page. Unfortunately, they were unorganized as before and I had to find out from Northrop and someone at CASA if I was to fly the flutter program or not.

In the end, I did all the flutter or vibration tests they wanted me to do. But, Don Murray, our Northrop engineer, wrote some comments regarding those tests and what exactly went on with CASA. We didn't clear a true technical flutter test and we were almost finished. Northrop was running out of money for the contract and I still had the spin tests to do.

During my second tour in Spain, Cynda, came over for a couple of weeks without the kids. She had hired a friend to stay at our house in Lancaster to watch over the kids while they were in school. This time, she already knew most of the Spanish friends, and I had a nice little flat very close to downtown Madrid. It was easier to keep her entertained than to entertain the whole family. She would stick her nose in a book and be happy for hours. Then it was out on the town every night. We would meet a group down in the second basement of the Euro International Hotel in downtown Madrid about midnight and disco dance till 2 a.m. You would see Spanish gentlemen come down there with some of the most gorgeous gals, one on each arm; and the escorted women would dance the night away with their man, all three at the same time. Our group, usually three or four couples, would all get up in a circle and dance together. It was a gas!

Like I said before, it was a tough job, but someone had to do it. The Spanish had a nonchalant attitude when it came time to discuss the spin tests. As a matter of fact, I was rather perturbed that they could be so indifferent about saving their airplane or my life. As we sat down to discuss the possibilities of loosing an airplane in an uncontrollable spin, I explained all the unrecoverable aspects of a spin test and what could happen if they did not install an auxiliary recovery device to save the plane. They listened and talked about the fact that they understood the dangers, but you could just see the thought patterns going around the table as they decided that it simply wouldn't matter if they lost the airplane; after all they had three more! I wanted to ask what about me? But, it is the same universally, the pilot is replaceable too.

So here I am again, with ole' Richard's head on the chopping block and my neck already in the vise. I am damned if I do, and damned if I don't. There were a few moments when I wanted to tell them to fly the spin test themselves, but I knew that would be a disaster when or if it ever happened. It wasn't going to get any better so I knew, I needed be very sure of this airplanes' maneuverability before I put it in a spin. The word was, the airplane won't spin, and my guess was that I had better make sure I could recover it if it did. We tried many ways in the program to make it spin and I was able to recover it each time. However, there were very strict limits on certain characteristics. We did *not* go past those limits. Later I heard someone got into an uncontrollable spin because of FOD in the airplane. It must have crashed but I never heard if the pilot was killed. I wasn't surprised at all as I had complained often about scrap material in the wing, like nuts, bolts, pieces of rivets, small chunks of material, all as a result of building the plane. They simply did not get it, that when the word 'clean' was mentioned it meant 'Foreign Object Damage' in the aircraft.

The other thing I had been sent to Spain for was the Farnborough Airshow outside of London. The Spanish people were very proud of their accomplishment and wanted the whole of Europe and the world to see their new 'jet baby'. They had four airplanes now and two were painted red and white and two were blue and white. They had assigned their pilot, Captain Verano, who had flown the plane to fly two shows. I was also contracted to fly two shows. This was part of my job for Northrop; so the two of us would rotate on our days to fly the plane. We each flew a CASA C-101 to London from Madrid. The Farnborough International Airshow has been world famous for years. And I was having a rush of adrenaline about getting to fly in this show.

Many of our Spanish friends and their wives were flown to London to promote the new CASA C-101. This was to be a real feather in my cap to fly in the Farnborough Airshow. Farnborough is the home of the Royal Aircraft Establishment in Hampshire, approximately 30 miles south west of central London. Verano and I were given white satin flying jackets to wear over our crisp new blue flying suits.

DICK, READY TO FLY IN THE FARNBOUGH AIRSHOW

The Spanish had set up a regular chalet for their guests and employees. King Juan Carlos and his Queen were in attendance at the chalet, in their own little 'cove' where the 'common folks' wouldn't bother them. Verano and I were treated like royalty too as we were the performers selling their product. The stage was set.

Cynda was flying in on Freddie Lakers flights to London and landing at Gatwick Airport a couple of days after I arrived with the C-101. We all were set up in hotels in London with transportation back and forth to Farnborough. So every other day I would fly a show, however we were required to be at the show and stay with the airplane for sales support, if we were not flying.

It was July, 1978, the Thursday before the show. We had been practicing our routines at Farnborough and as I came back to my hotel, I realized I had to take the train to Gatwick Airport to pick up Cynda. One might think it would be simple since English is spoken in England, to know how to do things once you get to the airport. But, believe me nothing was simple in London. I realized I was going to be a little late getting there; and she wouldn't have a clue where to go or how to get in touch with me.

Arriving thirty minutes late, I looked around for her, finally spotting her in a line of people waiting to exchange dollars to pounds. She didn't see me as she had her back to me. So I quietly slipped up behind her and asked in a muffled voice "Hey girlie will you sleep with me tonight?"

She jumped about a foot, and then she realized it was me. So it was back to London on the train which takes about an hour. We finally got her settled into our hotel room that was about the size of a postage stamp. She had a quick bath and changed to a sexy little cocktail dress and we were off to meet our Spanish friends for a fancy dinner at a French restaurant in London.

The next day she came to Farnborough for my air show demonstration. It was not my best day. The Spanish wives were more interested in shopping in London. So Cynda was relatively alone in the chalet, although there were Spaniards there as well. We had purchased a movie camera and she was checked out about the operation of it and had done quite well with her past talent of picture taking. However, as I took off to fly that day, she started the camera rolling and as we reviewed the film later we could not tell what I was doing. The camera was shaking so badly that half the time the airplane was not even in the picture. I guess she was just a little nervous (like Bettieann had been that day on the roof of the Northrop hangar in Palmdale) to watch me fly in this air show.

I didn't know what I was in for as I landed the airplane and headed for the Spanish chalet. The Queen was seriously waiting for me and as I came into the room, she grabbed me and planted a big kiss on my mouth. Cynda, stood off at one side and watched, she seemed just slightly peeved to see that she wasn't going to be the one that got to kiss me. I felt obliged to offer the Queen my arm escorting her to their privately reserved area. She continued fawning over me. And as I looked to the opposite corner of the chalet at Cynda, I saw her standing there looking confused. She was already mad because the announcer had mistakenly called out Verano as the pilot of the C-101 taking off. I wasn't too happy either as he really didn't have a very good show. Later, I learned that the review of my show in the Aviation Week was quite complimentary. Why I didn't say something to the Queen and call Cynda over to introduce her was more than I could explain to Cynda later.

We were there six hectic days, and then I returned the airplane to Spain to finish the program and get ready to return to the United States. Cynda had flown over on Freddie Lakers Airline, and it was a package deal. She had to stay 10 days. Therefore, she signed up to take a tour; it would include an old castle, the Oxford University, the Ann Hathaway thatched home and finish at the historical Stratford on Avon village. This last part of her trip turned out to be impressive as she would tell all our friends at home about seeing the play called "Measure for Measure" at the Shakespeare theatre that evening.

She was with a tour group of mixed vacationers from all parts of Europe, some spoke English but she was alone most of the time. They first visited an old castle outside of London that had a horrible dungeon with all of the paraphernalia used to torture women who were considered guilty of 'naughty things'. These grotesque pieces were exhibited on long tables and hung on walls. Then it was on to Oxford University with a grand tour and the Ann Hathaway cottage with six foot ceilings. They arrived in Stratford on Avon where Beef Wellington was served to the group at a nearby restaurant. The group's accommodations were at the 400 year old White Swan Hotel. Now Cynda was a tall five feet, two inches and she claimed she could reach the ceilings as they were only six feet high. History tells us people in England in those very early years were fairly small in stature.

The real thrill for her was the play that night at the Shakespeare Theatre. For those of you who might not know the story of "Measure for Measure", here is a brief summary. It seems there were a couple of teens who got into trouble, the girl became pregnant and the boy was sentenced to death by the English Lord. They put the boy in prison and when it came time to behead him, the friar and the executioner decided to substitute a murderer's head for the boy's head. At the point when they let the murderer out of his cell to behead him, he escaped from the two and started running and jumping over things on stage, they chased him for a time on stage and finally caught him. Doesn't sound too exciting to me, however, I forgot to tell Cynda's punch line. The prisoner was *stark naked* and according to her rendition, quite a manly specimen! It would seem to me she would have seen enough of a manly specimen during the past six days to not be so ruffled.

Cynda's last night in England on this ten day whirlwind was another adventure. As the tour bus arrived back in London late on a Friday evening, she found the tour office closed. The tourists all left the bus and scattered like ants leaving her stranded in the middle of the block not knowing what to do. She had purchased several items and had her overnight bag, making it impossible for her to carry all of them. Frustrated, she asked a young man to help her get to the corner to hail a taxi, but little did she realize hailing a cabby on Friday evening in London was near to impossible.

As the sun began to fade, she began to feel panicky. A slight rain had started and she had been on this corner nearly an hour trying to flag a cab. Her flight left early the next morning and she had to get to Victoria Station, catch the train to Gatwick Airport, check in before 11 p.m. and then go to her motel by bus. Things were beginning to look grim. As she told me, she stood there praying to God when an older gentleman tapped her on the shoulder. He was a short rotund little man, dressed in a three-piece suit with a bright gold watch chain across his chest. He handed her his card and asked where she was trying to go.

After Cynda told him her story, he then took her back down to the middle of the block, got on the double-decker bus carrying her suitcase...leaving her to carry the packages. He explained that this bus would take them to Charring Cross where he would be able to get her a cab. When they arrived at Charring Cross, he quickly put her in the taxi, gave the cabby some money. Then he instructed the cabby to get a porter to help her get her large piece of luggage out of the check room at Victoria Train Station and put her on the correct train to Gatwick. She had no idea what was going on, Mr. McClendon, had given the cabby all the necessary instructions. Then he turned to her and commented that she had his card, and when or if she got back to the United States okay, would she please write to him in Glasgow, Scotland, and let him know. Cynda kept in touch with him for a couple of years. Then one day a small white envelope came from Scotland and it was his secretary telling her that Mr. McClendon had passed away. Cynda always said he was her Guardian Angel.

Victoria Station is a nightmare if you are a stranger, as there must be 15 tracks for trains, maybe more. There was a line of people a block long waiting to get their checked luggage. The cabby quickly got a porter, gave him the luggage ticket and some of the money. The porter went into the check room himself and retrieved her large piece of luggage. From that point, he put Cynda on Train No. 11 to Gatwick near the rear of the car and told her, that when the train started slowing down, she must get all her luggage and packages and put them in the end of the car near the exit steps. There would be a high platform when they came into the airport terminal. When the train started slowing down and finally was moving very slowly near the platform, she must shove her suitcases off and jump off with her packages! The train *did not stop* at Gatwick! So she did just as he said, and by the time she got to her hotel room that night, it was 11 o'clock. No food had been available since lunch that day; and the hotel kitchen was closed by the time she checked in. She had to leave the next morning before the kitchen opened. Cynda was getting pretty hungry by the time she arrived at Gatwick that morning. There wasn't any time to get breakfast as her departure flight had changed; and they started boarding soon after she arrived. Good old Freddie Lakers served a bountiful breakfast on the flight. I think she was very glad to get home; she had had enough adventure for a while.

So Spain was great while it lasted, and we kept in touch with our friends year after year. Then gradually we started loosing touch. However, the memories of adventure would never be forgotten. In 1994 we went back for a visit, but the glory dew was off the flower and even though we had several friends who hosted us, they couldn't know what I had done in the U.S.A. on the Tacit Blue program, because it was still top secret. I realized that those friends were riding high on my performance on the C-101 back in the days of testing their airplane, but sadly, life never stays the same.

CHAPTER 14

TACIT BLUE AND THE UNKNOWN

✦

Sometimes, things literally fall into place. Maybe it is luck or maybe it is God's plan for our lives. One never knows why or how, whether it is fate or karma. But for me it was the chance of a life time; the 'ole' opportunity guy was knocking at my door again.

Like Captain Ahab, I was going to get my encounter with the great white whale. Unlike Ahab though, I would triumph. I would fare with the Tacit Blue like Captain Nemo of the Nautilus. Still our group became known as the 'Whalers'. People would ask us if 'the Whale' really existed and we would answer, "Oh yes the whale exists."

I'm not quite sure why I was selected because all the information, all the activities for Tacit Blue were classified, so people didn't talk about this project. We weren't allowed to sit around and discuss the project. But, I happened to be walking across the parking lot one day and Steve Smith yelled to me and we stopped to talk. It was December, 1978. He and I had worked together on the F-5 spin tests and other Northrop projects. And Steve said, "Are you interested in doing something else?"

I asked, "What do you mean?"

"Well, are you through traveling around the world with the F-5 Sales group?" he asked.

When I said, "Yes".

He said, "Give me a call. I've got something you might be interested in."

Of course, that's all anybody could ever say in those days is 'give me a call'. So, I waited a couple of weeks, Steve never called me and I got to thinking well, things are very slow in the F-5 business. We had gone all over the world with the F-5 demonstrating the airplane to foreign military groups. The future looked much brighter in a classified program, and you don't leave the U.S.A.

With Steve's remark about a call, I decided to do just that. I was very curious to find out what he might have been talking about that day in the parking lot. He was very encouraging and said, "I'll tell you what Dick, come over to this building…" and (gave me the number and a specific date). I thought, well, what can I loose?

Sometimes you don't know what you are getting into but intrigue seems to drive you on. So I went to meet him and was briefed into the program. Steve had obviously taken care of the fact that this guy's coming into the program and we've got to brief him. Otherwise I wouldn't have been told anything. At the time he was Program Manager for this new secret project at Northrop, but I didn't know his position then. I had no way of knowing why they had selected me; however, I had established an incredible reputation for the 'high angle of attack pilot' with all those spin tests. It was going to be another 'aha' day for sure and I was up there on cloud nine again thinking about the prospects of flying something so incapable of flight!

After Steve's briefing I knew I was going to be involved. Once they open the door and take you in, they lock you in with no intention of letting you go again. You are only aware of the subject you are being briefed on, and at that time you may not even know the whole scope of the project. In fact it is so compartmentalized that your phase of business is not anyone else's business, even though you may be working on the same project.

After getting indoctrinated into the Tacit Blue program I was designated the Project Test Pilot and Site Manager for Tacit Blue. Getting into a project like this took considerable time for screening and investigative procedures. During the time it took to get me my clearances, I was learning the ropes of the operation and finding out just what I was *not to do.* Surprisingly, I was put through several training sessions and rigorous self discipline protection practices. There were different levels of security. Some of the people I worked with only had the one clearance, and then some had more than one or several. Although I never asked, I assumed I had several, as I was asked to contribute my expertise on different classified programs. So as I would leave one project, doors automatically locked behind me. After a hand scan, I would walk into another area to work on the next project.

On one occasion, I inadvertently left my briefcase on the tarmac and walked away several steps. Immediately two armed guards approached the area to corral the briefcase and one came up to me and said, "Mr. Thomas will you please pick up your briefcase."

It was a real eye-opener and embarrassing for me to have made a mistake like that. My initial responsibilities were to give input wherever it was needed. This kind of stuff was right up my alley, and I loved every minute of it. At this stage of the game I discovered, Skip Hickey, an associate from Wright-Pat, the government's side, was also on this project as their Chief Engineer. We had worked on the crazy X-21 together back at Edwards in 1965. I was happy to see Skip again; we had a great time working together as he was a no-nonsense engineer.

That interview I spoke of earlier, with Major Ruthie Williamson at Wright-Patterson, lasted three to four hours. Skip and I reminisced over those hectic hours we spent in the simulator trying to sort out multiple control problems that were the very essence of the critically unstable Tacit Blue.

I think the Major was enjoying our banter, and I know Cynda was learning a lot about things she had never heard me mention at home. So you might say she finally discovered information that probably answered a lot of her misgivings about my strange behavior at home during those 'black world' years. The wives gave a lot for us guys who couldn't come home during the week, and couldn't say where we had been. Just consider it the same as military life during war, 'it is secret, I can't tell'.

As Skip reiterated at that meeting, his job in the case of the Tacit Blue was to make this funny looking shape fly and that was it. He had no business knowing what the low observable characteristics of the airplane were and he didn't learn that until he had been Chief Engineer for a while. In other words it's what you need to know to do the job. Our reminiscing continued on and on for Major Ruth's benefit.

You could be working on the airplane and not know anything more than the little niche you were doing. It might have retarded the program's advancement somewhat because there was no interchange back and forth unless authorized. But, this system insured top security, and that was the first priority.

When I came into the program the airplane was in the early stages, a plywood mock-up. In fact, they were outlining the windows. There was still a great flexibility in the configuration, like how high or where should the windows be. I would sit in the cockpit and say things like, 'boy, this is a very wide cockpit and I can't see out very well'. I was given a lot of input since I would be the first one flying this weird craft. There were several design engineers who fought the battle of trying to get the pilot the best visibility. And of course, the electronics people or the low observables people wanted the minimum. They would have put no windows in the cockpit at all, if they had their way.

I became involved in the actual flight profile, as to when you would do the test flights on Tacit Blue. There was a group of people that actually mapped out this whole program through the envelope, to the speed point, and to the load point. Then we found out that we were spending too much time and too much money doing all of these test conditions. So it was back to the drawing board to reduce the size of the program. After that there were only four or five of us that got together and went back through the program chopping and cutting. And eventually, we realized we could get the qualified data even with a sizeable reduction in the program.

After looking at the whole picture; we kept what was really required to prove that this aircraft was flight worthy within the envelope that we needed. As it turned out, natural events would have prevented us from going with the first program anyway, because of some serious characteristics that were not going to pass the flight tests. For instance, speed wise we had limited conditions. I don't think that the inlet… or, I can't say because stuff like that is a sensitivity problem as far as security is concerned. But if you went faster than a certain MACH number and pulled Gs, the engines would stall. Tacit Blue was never intended to go supersonic anyway. However it was reduced from what the original speed envelope called for. It would have proven out that way anyway. As I found out later, you would start a dive and if you went over the Mach number by one or two hundreds and pulled up to slow it down, you'd hear *BANG! BANG! BANG!* in the engines. A little unnerving I must admit.

Skip Hicky was quick to explain to Major Williamson that at the time I came in, the basic configuration of the airplane was determined. They had the aerodynamic data, the airplane was totally unstable, it was a 'squirrel' and it was the worst. They were at the point where they had an idea what the flight control system ought to be, but needed pilots to get in, fly it, and evaluate it to help them optimize it; and that's when I came in. He paid me a nice compliment by saying he was real glad to see me as he had worked with me before. Anyway, this was the renewing of our friendship with many nights to follow in the simulator, working out the kinks in the flight control system.

It seemed like endless hours spent in that simulator…sometimes until twelve o'clock at night. The engineers were making up these ridiculous tests for us and we spent what seemed like months doing everything conceivable to make it fly. My greatest concern was to be able to reach everything in the cockpit that I needed in flight. During this same time, the engineers had me working on the B-2 simulator also. I would work four hours on the Tacit Blue simulator and then four hours on other projects. Consequently, I had a tremendous amount of input that influenced the design, the configuration and the shape of 'things'.

Again, Skip was quick to say that I was always in somebody else's office either learning about the airplane or making a suggestion as to where this or that ought to be. His comment was that I had touched many things in Tacit Blue, especially from the standpoint of the flight control system. As Skip continued he told the Major just what I was faced with; that the airplane was unstable in pitch and yaw right at the landing configuration which was around eight degrees angle of attack. I agreed. He went on…since it was unstable on both axes--with only two sets of fins to stabilize it…(with the way the flight control system was set up)… you would park it in one axis while you controlled it in the other axis. Confusing isn't it? That's all the surface power that you had, so we devised a 'simple test' where we had to land in turbulence because the site was known for having some turbulence problems. Yeh, there's that 'simple test' jargon again!

Skip's comment was, "Just when Dick ran the airplane out; we would get a ten-foot per second gust and it would happen right in the flare. Sometimes it would be in pitch and sometimes it would be in yaw. Dick's job was to 'catch' the airplane and land it".

We spent many a night in the simulator and that was the easy part. Another problem with the airplane was that it had a very strong pitch-up tendency around twelve degrees angle of attack. So you had a four-degree margin of error! Then the airplane was set up with an auxiliary pitch recovery device, which was a board about the size of a long table in the bottom of the airplane. We were constantly working this design between two extremes, being able to land, and still being able to have enough control power to handle the stall and we had to figure out a compromise between the two. And that was the job! Did he say, just a 'simple test'?

As Major Ruthie listened, Skip remembered on, "We had Dick in the simulator fighting the system, night after night, hour after hour, and there are a couple of excerpts that I seem to remember. One night, we thought we almost had the gust fixed. Dick had given us pilot ratings of about three or four, and we finally gave him another ten-foot per second gust. He lost the thing bigger than hell and Dave Maunder, Jay Strange and I (Skip) are all there, so frustrated, when Dick jokes, 'Now guys, don't get discouraged 'cause you found *a pimple on Miss America's ass.* We'll get it solved.' He cracked us up lots of times with his wit and jokes. Then one night we gave him a gust in yaw and Dick is working like hell trying to catch it with the rudder pedals. After we stopped, I (Skip) said, Dick, I think your thighs are still smoking!"

"We had a lot of fun in the simulator, even though there were lots of long hours and nights of sorting out… that he was doing for us. But Dick would agree that is the only thing that saved his ass in flying the 'thing'!"

I did agree with Skip. All of these control problems were not easy to solve, but I guess they appeared easy once they were all put together. Had we not pursued what we did about solving the ten-foot-per-second gust and so forth, we would have been in serious trouble. We actually ran into two phenomena in flight, which are rare, in fact you really don't want to run into them. One of them was at thirty-six thousand feet or something like that…high altitude and I had a chase airplane. The chase plane penetrated the area that I wanted to fly through; and in order to do it I had to say 'it was okay, the turbulence is not too high to fly through there'. We flew through it and we hit a gust that 'the upset' was, I don't know, probably fifty feet per second. It was an 'abrupt step' input from the control system and it just all went 'bing', then we went through it just fine.

The really bad problem occurred when we were on an approach landing. We expected that if we ran into a gust that exceeded fifty feet per second, there'd be no way to control the airplane. But everybody said, not to worry, there's no such thing in nature as a fifty-foot per second gust. So on final approach, you've seen these dust devils on the desert? Well, one of those apparently was sitting right there off the end of the runway at about two hundred feet and you can't fly to avoid them. I didn't even see it. But at about two hundred feet or so, I hit this thing and it drove one of the actuators all the way to the physical metal stop and it hit hard enough that I heard it up in the cockpit.

I guess it traveled up through the structure. As near as we could figure that was a fifty-foot per second gust. The other really unnerving thing was there's the analog type of signals which will trace you a smooth curve and there are digital signals which make their little step marks as they go on out. It turned out that there was a by-pass, that under a condition, if you got a certain type of signal in the digital to analog conversion, it would not adhere to this electrical stop. All the actuators had electrical stops, in other words, they had sensors in the system that would say, okay, it's traveling too fast towards the end of the actuator and we've got to stop it and it would put in a stop signal. Well, this was one of those by-pass things that you get in computers that allowed it to by-pass the digital stop by going through the analog tract. Nobody knew it was there because we had never had any reason to check it. The engineering people had checked all of it and nobody thought of anything like that being there. So on final approach, coming down, all of a sudden I hear this 'wham*!*' And, I thought well nothing happened and I'm still progressing on. I wondered if I had hit a fence post or telephone pole.

Nobody could see anything wrong with the airplane, but of course, we're on final approach, so I went ahead and landed…best thing to do. When they got the data and started looking at it, they found that the actuator, through its analog signal failure, had allowed the piston in the actuator to travel all the way to the end of the cylinder. It hit the end with a force hard enough that I heard it up in the cockpit, fifty feet away or so. It actually showed that '*the pimple on Miss America's ass*' had not been cured!

Skip was not about to take blame for this and came back with his own story. He had been there for my first flight on Tacit Blue. He claimed that on the first flight he was watching the tails and as I came down close to the flare, both tails did a very large, abrupt trailing edge down and trailing edge back. He said he thought, '*holy cow*'…*you got one on the first flight.* That first flight was another story of its own.

Well, I might have gotten a gust that big on landing; there was so much confusion on the first flight. I'm sure that all those hours on the control system were worth every hour. Not only was Tacit Blue an original, saved for the Wright-Patterson Air Force Museum, but the system also saved my hide. After the first flight, Skip was reassigned and that was the last time he saw the airplane until it was shipped to Wright-Patterson Air Force Museum, Dayton, Ohio.

Cynda got a few questions in too, and she asked, "Did these incidents happen because the engines were installed inside the fuselage?"

My answer was a little vague, and I had to blame it on George Grant because he was the ornery guy who designed the inlets. George was a friend of mine and we were always needling each other. There were certain factors that caused this to happen. Sure enough George claims he knew that this was the case; that it would happen. And even if it did, he didn't come forward and make a big deal to worry us. As he said there was no reason to make a big issue of it. We pilots would have discovered it. And, as you may perceive, the problem really didn't matter as the engineers would have just declared a MACH limit.

Well, Tacit Blue's first flight happened on February 5, 1982. A fateful day of history making started that day and if I had been asked how the first flight had gone, I might have blown it again. I probably would have said something like… 'Right after lift-off I nearly *crapped my pants! *$# because it didn't even fly like the simulator* and in addition our air to ground data system failed. Therefore no one could do anything except yell at me to *abort!*'

FIRST FLIGHT OF TACIT BLUE, DICK THOMAS, TEST PILOT

There was a story going around about the night before the first flight. It seems Vice President John Cashen's version went something like this. He said I was so up-tight that night that I couldn't sleep. So, the two of us shot hoops for about an hour and then I had a couple of beers before I could get to sleep. That wasn't the way I remember it but, maybe that was the way it was. Usually I could put my head on the pillow, close my eyes and be asleep. There had been some delays previously with problems on the 'whale' and we had postponed the flight. But I was ready and willing, in fact anxious to get this bird into the air.

So on my first flight out…it's another one of those 'gee-whiz' stories. There is all this vast array of sophisticated data and data acquisition system. The engineers are sitting breathlessly down in the ready room and they are watching all these squiggles. All of us expected certain things and there was a rule that I could not continue a flight if the ground engineers couldn't monitor the data. So going down the runway, everything's proceeding fine. At lift off the main gear comes off the ground and at that moment, the data stopped transmitting to ground control. Everybody on the ground is electronically 'blind'. The on-board recorders are still working and are still doing their job and recording the data, but none of the engineers on the ground can tell what is going on. They start yelling, *'ABORT, ABORT, ABORT, ABORT!'* Well, hell, at this point I am too high and too far down the runway to put it back down.

During the take-off, the Tacit Blue didn't know whether she was going to fly or become a porpoise. After all, she had been designated 'the Whale' and as we all know, most whales can't fly. But during those long hours in the simulator, that was our job, to make whales fly; and soon I would find out, if we had done our job or not. There were so many factions to think about on this first flight and as I became airborne, I realized I was not in complete charge of this weird duck. She began her porpoise movement as I was gaining speed and altitude over the runway. This was not what I had planned and as I tried to correct each dip and peak, I realized the computer was also trying to get this 'bathtub' stabilized. It happened about the same time, as the control room was screaming for me to 'abort'. Now I realized there was no way I could 'abort' at this very point without killing myself, and I took the option to live.

Normally, the pilot would follow procedure, but I am sitting up there and I had finally got the airplane under control and it's going along fine. Here I am trying to figure out if I am putting an input in or what, and they are still yelling 'abort'. (Interjecting here, the reason for the disruption in ground control information was the failure of the coaxial switch fuse at lift off.)

There was one thing I didn't do; I didn't call what page on the notes for all the people on the ground to go to. I presumed since they were telling me to abort, that everybody knew what we were doing. I just went to the 'abort' page. But afterward, there were complaints from the ground crew that since they didn't have data, they didn't know what page to go to. There was a check list and I followed the procedure which gave us a pattern to go around, do certain things and land. Actually, the first flight continued to be about 20 minutes and upon landing, we had the first incident as Skip said with the ten-foot per minute gust. Was it a successful flight? In my books, when you take off and land without hurting yourself, it is a successful flight.

The problem with the whining engineers in the control room was kind of strange, it was rather ridiculous as someone was groaning and moaning because they didn't have data and 'I' didn't tell them what page to go to next. These higher level people are used to having someone reach over and turn to the proper page.

Once when I was telling Cynda about the first flight, she asked what would have happened if you had crashed? I told her that they always had two completely staffed Medi-vac helicopters flying in the chase support group on *every* flight for the worst case scenario.

Major Ruthie wanted to know why we nicknamed Tacit Blue "the whale". It was one of those things I couldn't claim, but someone told me I had called it that. The morning I walked into the hangar to fly the first flight. Those cocky maintenance guys had stuck a happy face on the aircraft, it had a great big smile and it had eyes. It looked like a whale.

TACIT BLUE VIEW FROM THE TOP

Across the tarmac was this 'other' aerospace corporation; their engineers and pilots were all betting this creature wouldn't fly. In fact, they were so interested in my first flight of Tacit Blue; they gathered up 4 x 8 plywood sheets, painted them in capital letters with a display and hung them across their hangar doors to read: "*GOOD LUCK, CAPTAIN AHAB!*"

It was the most ridiculous idea, that working across the runway from each other, we were not to see what Brand X was doing, and they were to keep their eyes closed also when Brand Y was going to fly their first flight. In fact, Cynda, worked for Lockheed in flight test at this time. They had a bunch of guys making strange comments to her sometimes. She had no idea what they were talking about, as I never talked about the 'black world' to her. She had not realized we were all at the same location.

Anyway, to get back to the first flight, when I came in for my first flight landing, the people from Brand X had turned the 4 x 8 plywood sheets over and they read: "*CONGRATULATIONS, CAPTAIN NEMO!*" Meaning I had conquered the 'beast'. There were pictures taken of their hangar and years later Cynda's friends from Lockheed promised to get her copies but it never happened.

There may have been an incident that I called it a whale. There was a landing where I was told to get the vehicle on the ground immediately, or as soon as possible. We had had rain and it began to freeze. There were spots on the runway and the chase pilot and I got in the car and drove out to check to see how much water and ice were on the runway. We decided it was okay to go ahead with the mission, and so I went. Then I got this call interrupting the test and the reason to abort.

When I came in and landed, everything was going fine. Tacit Blue rolled very fast and you had a long distance to kill the ground speed on the craft. Consequently, I am trying to stop, but there was no anti-lock braking system so you had to be very careful not to skid the tires above a hundred knots. If you did you'd probably blow them and that was what happened to me. I had hit a big puddle of water, got the brakes on, then went into another puddle of water, but I didn't get off the brakes good enough. So one wet tire went flat right there on the runway and the other one had a great big bald spot where it had slid but not quite blown. Everything is frantic now; you're trying to get the airplane off the runway, to clear for another plane to land. You can't tow it with a blown tire, so a lot of crew came out and changed the tire right there, very, very quickly.

So Skip is telling a different story that the tower is telling me to, 'please stop' and I'm telling them I am trying to but 'Shamu' is heading for the water!' And, he tells Ruthie, it is perfectly in context with who I am. But, I can't deny I said it, there is one thing I do know; that it was not a taxi test.

There was a reason Tacit Blue was so hard to stop. The wheels and brakes were made for a smaller airplane, and in fact, many parts were confiscated from the F-5 airplane to save money on the program. You never got enough capability from this off-the-shelf equipment; you rely a lot on the skill of the driver. Fortunately, for me I was quite acquainted with this ornery 'whale' and I was able to keep it from drastic destruction. On several occasions I had to go clear to the end of the runway on landings, then turn around and taxi back to my area.

Since I was the Northrop Project Pilot, I was always the first one to fly the aircraft. Actually, I flew the first four flights before the Air Force pilot was allowed to fly it. During those first four flights, I and the engineering team worked out a number of serious technical problems that made it relatively safer for the Air Force pilots that would be flying starting with the fifth flight. Each engineering change was flown by the contractor pilot first and then by the Air Force pilot. The Northrop Corporation was totally responsible for the program and the airplane. There were 136 flights approved by the Air Force but we were able to accomplish our objectives with only 135 flights by the end of the program. I had flown about 60% of the total flights and our team of Northrop stars was able to impress even the Air Force's highest ranking generals. It was amazing that the secret was so well kept with the Northrop gang, you'd see them downtown and nobody would act like they even knew each other. It was years afterward that the story finally broke. In fact a comment was made at my retirement party by Steve Smith, "Finally, a test pilot that can keep a secret!"

During the Tacit Blue program, I also worked on the simulator for the B-2 bomber, the advanced technology attack airplane and the attack technology fighter which became the F-23. However, Lockheed won the award for the ATF which was the F-22. Initially, I was the only pilot working on the B-2 simulator from 1978 to 1982. I continued working on the B-2 simulator until I quit flying in 1985. With all this work in the simulator on different projects, I would go into the simulator a lot of times at four o'clock in the afternoon and I wouldn't come out of there until twelve o'clock at night. There were several totally separate programs, but I was one of the people working on more than one. You would get through flying one project and leave that one…go into another secret project and start all over on it.

We have another good story regarding pantyhose. There was one time when Terry Bolsted went around the facility gathering up all the pantyhose he could find. We had a situation in Tacit Blue where we had an electrical contactor burn up right in the airplane. Fortunately it was right after I got out of the plane. Don Cornell was about to make the next flight and it started right then and burned.

What we found out was that the air compressor was blowing shavings…or very small pieces of aluminum into the cockpit. This stuff was going through the cockpit environmental control system, and some of it apparently collected. The contactor was in the cockpit. Normally we wouldn't put it in the cockpit but for this particular plane, that is where it was put. You know, you're always doing things in experimental airplanes that you wouldn't do for a normal operation. It seems that enough of this chaff blew into the control system that it shorted out the contactor. The blue lights in the cockpit got really brilliant and all of a sudden the contactor burst into flame right on the spot. It got our attention quickly, for if something like this was to happen during a flight; that could be fatal!

We were trying everything we could to prevent any reoccurrence, so to prove our point they put the pantyhose over the inlet pipes in the cockpit to filter them. Don't ask where they got the pantyhose; none of the guys wore them that I know of. I guess this is just another top secret!

It was 1985, the Tacit Blue project was complete and I was looking forward to just being put in a rather nice managerial position at Northrop. I had completely reveled in the Air Force's laurels and compliments on the success of the project. Even though the project was still top secret and would not be talked about publicly for maybe years to come, I felt that certain people in high positions knew what I personally had done for Northrop and the program.

The following year when I went for my yearly flight physical, I received some disappointing news. I had a slight click in my heart and I guess the old rheumatic fever tick had come back to haunt me. When I left the doctor's office, I knew I was done and that my flying career was over. Oh sure I could fly commercial or private aircraft, but no more test flying. It was a hard career knock and left me feeling depressed.

The general public and Northrop's regular employees had no idea what I had done for Northrop or even what I had accomplished. Even my own family had no knowledge of the 'black world' flying. There were several of the B-2 employees who had been on Tacit Blue and they were well aware of my accomplishments. But, I couldn't talk to them, it was strictly my own nightmare and I would have to deal with it the best way I could. I was only 56 and I had a lot of valuable experience and knowledge that the company could use. But I had been in the 'black world' for eight years, and a lot of changes had taken place in upper management back in Northrop's main plant. Unfortunately for me, I wasn't a 'player' and I found out that no one really cared who I was or what I had done. It was a very rude awakening.

I felt like the little boy on the outside looking in, it was a horrible experience to come down to after the euphoria of the great success we had just accomplished on Tacit Blue. After all, these people at Northrop were working on the B-2; and I had personally helped win this contract for Northrop. 'No Tacit Blue, No B-2' was the motto that would eventually come to the public. But it would take another ten years before I would get any recognition for contributing anything!

In fact when the B-2 rollout was presented at Palmdale, almost every cat and dog was invited. However, yours truly and my wife were not so much as considered worthy. It wasn't even thought of that I might have had anything to do with Northrop's B-2 at all. Bill Aplas who had worked on Tacit Blue invited Cynda to his house to watch the rollout on his TV, so she went. There were a couple other guys there that were involved with Tacit Blue. None of them were invited to the affair either. As a matter of fact, I sat on a bale of hay and watched from the side of the hangar.

Then that fateful day that the B-2 pilot taxied the plane, I made the comment to some of the guys watching. He better be careful with his speed when he taxies or he will become airborne and won't be able to stop it. Those words were prophetic as we watched him speed down the runway, the nose wheel lifted off a foot or so, and then the B-2 became uncontrollable. The plane left the runway and got stuck in the softened tarmac and dirt. If I had been the pilot, I would have been mortified and probably fired. Later, I was told by several of the 'Whalers' crew they wanted me to taxi the B-2 the first time, but Northrop would not hear of it. The fact that I knew the airplane as well as or better than the ones flying it, didn't matter. It was just another political farce.

The story at Aplas's house as I heard it was, when Cynda saw the airplane, she made the comment that Dick was probably eating his heart out because he didn't get to fly this one. But ole Bill, came back with this little quip, "Are you kidding, your man has flown a lot more hairier stuff than this, just to make sure the B-2 would fly. Hell, we put pieces of metal, nuts and bolts together, and he would go out and fly it. Then he would land and we would change the configuration and stick something else on the damn thing. And Dick would take off again and make that thing fly too. He could fly a damn bathtub or a cardboard box if he had to. I can say this; you don't need to feel sorry for Dick, that guy has seven-pound balls!"

That was a quote that Cynda never forgot and repeated it whenever she had the right audience. The sad part to me was when the B-2 did fly; there was never a mention of Dick Thomas or anything I had ever done on or in the simulator. For a long time I was the first and only pilot working in the B-2 simulator back in the early days. Thank you very much!

It wasn't until after the unveiling in 1996, that I received any recognition on Tacit Blue. But I must say the guys who worked with me out in that remote area were some of the most dedicated men I have ever had the pleasure of being around. They all had my back on this operation as far as I could tell. In fact here is a poem that was written by James (Jim) E. Coleman at the end of our program. Now to explain first about something in the poem, that little three cornered black job that Lockheed built was flying around near us and we referred to it as 'the *HORNY TOAD*'. I and some of the other pilots flew the *F-15 EAGLE* and *F-16* to keep current. Then, of course, I flew '*the WHALE*' and my call sign was '*Bandit 89*' so when you read the poem, you will understand some of the language a little better.

TRIBUTE TO ALL THE WHALERS

There is a place, or so I've heard
I really don't believe a single word.
It's out in the desert, or so they say
Across the line real far away,
A place where EAGLES seldom stray.
It's cold and dirty and way up high
Up where the mountains scrape the sky,
But it's a place of magic and wonder
For on a clear day, in the sky there's Thunder!
I've heard it whispered in a sigh

That it's a place where 'WHALES' can fly,
And 'HORNY TOADS' not landlocked bound
Streak through the air faster than sound.
And on a bright day way up high
You might even see a 'BANDIT' in the sky.
Strange men come here, they leave their home
And in this desert for months they roam.
Each day they go and risk their lives
They leave their children and leave their wives.
They test by day and toil by night,
They do the job till it's done right.
They seek not fortune, nor seek they gold
They have a story that may never be told.
They do the work that must be done
They fight a war that must be won.
America's strength through technology
Is what is keeping free men free.
So if you ever hear about this place
Please hope it exists in time and space
For what they do there can't be told
But freedom's light they there uphold.

Written by J.E. Coleman, an honorable 'Whaler'

The best of a man sometimes comes out in somber poems telling the truth about their gut feelings. In my opinion, Jim expressed truth in his words and the *Whalers* reading this could easily get choked up over a few truthful words. Jim passed away a few years back but his memory still lives on in the hearts of his *Whaler-buddies.*

◆   ◆   ◆

DIVERSION OF DUTY

During this same period, I was fortunate enough to steal away on a few week-ends with a good friend aboard his sailboat. Mike Kennedy was one of the crew station engineers at the main plant in Hawthorne. I'd always had a fascination with sailing and the intrinsic similarities sailing had with flying.

As a test pilot, one of my jobs was to review and discuss any and all proposed changes in the cockpit with respect to ergonomics, controls and displays. I would make frequent trips to Hawthorne for this purpose, which was usually followed by lunch in the Tech Center cafeteria with old friends, Jack Farley, Larry Green and Mike Kennedy. Our conversation would inevitably turn to Mike's 29 foot Ericson sailboat, which he spent his leisure time racing.

Invariably the subject of his racing would pique my interest. I had so many questions and he would do his best to answer but finally he said if I really wanted to understand what it was all about I should come out and crew for him. An island race was coming up in a few weeks and Mike welcomed me to come along. It would be an over-nighter; we would race over to Long Point on Santa Catalina Island on Saturday and then race back on Sunday. I couldn't say no.

Early on a Saturday morning, I observed; while the other crew members broke out the sails, rigged the sheets and readied to get under way. There are no ropes on a sailboat. There are dock and other miscellaneous lines; there are sheets that are led from the clews (corners) of the sails through blocks (pulleys) to winches and there are halyards that hoist the sails; no ropes.

This was a new experience for me and I was excited to be involved. We motored the boat out to the start area, what is known as the middle breakwater. The start line is set up as closely perpendicular to the wind as possible and between a flag on the race committee boat and a flag, or pin as they call it, in the water some distance away as determined by the number of boats and their lengths.

After a series of visual and sound signals, the first class of boats cross the line and are off and away, followed in five minute intervals by subsequent classes as determined by size and/or speed; the bigger and faster boats starting first. One of the first things that became glaringly apparent, as we left the harbor and headed into the open sea was that speed is relative. In a fighter jet, doing .85 Mach at thirty-five thousand feet, you really have no real sense of how fast you are going without looking at the airspeed indicator. But when you have two or more boats in close proximity to one another, 'a half of a knot' difference in boat speed can be white knuckling.

This new adventure turned me into an enthusiastic kid again. Going over was into the wind or 'going to weather' as they say; meaning that the main and head sails were close hauled and carefully trimmed such that you were sailing as close to or as high on the wind as possible. This was key because with the current and possible wind shifts, what you didn't want was to get close to the island and find that you had to tack your way back to the finish line. As it turned out, we did petty well and corrected out with a second place over all.

Having finished the race, we dropped the sails, tidied up the boat and motored into Whites Landing to pick up a mooring. They were expecting us and in no time at all the shore boats arrived to take us into Avalon. Now, it was party time, where we spent the evening dining, partaking of spirits and recounting the day's event with our competitors; some believable, some not.

Over the next few months, I made several of these races with Mike, accompanied a few times by his wife Anita. She was an avid sailor and loved racing, always claiming the boat was hers. Unfortunately, Anita was diagnosed with breast cancer and Mike lost her in 1985. His life changed then and he sold his boat and took up flying. I will always be grateful to Mike and Anita for having provided another dimension to my life that most probably would not otherwise have been afforded me.

After being gone during the entire week from 4 a.m. on Monday to 7 p.m. on Friday, on my secret job, Cynda became a little testy at my wanting to be gone on a sailing race for the weekend. But in July, 1983, during those hectic days of Tacit Blue, our friends from PAX River Test Pilot School, Wyn and Dick Adams invited us to take a holiday with them aboard their 44 ft. CSY cutter, the Wyn-A-Sue. Cynda was absolutely thrilled about the prospects of sailing in the Caribbean on their yacht. I certainly dreamed of having the time off too, but I found that breaking the stride in a secret program, of which you are the chief pilot, difficult.

It was the year of our 25th wedding anniversary and I had been on the 'black world' program since 1978. Before that I was gone to Spain six months in 1977 then another four months in 1978 when I returned to the U.S.A. to go into the 'black program'. I had literally been gone most of the time from 1977 through 1983 and things were a little ragged around the edges at home. Cynda had put her foot down and it was go---or don't go, but she was going! So the guy in charge and I, decided I could go.

Wyn and Cynda had enjoyed golfing together while we were at PAX River, even though Cynda wasn't much of a golfer (pregnant as she was). We had been their house guest in D.C. on occasion and enjoyed their hospitality. The Adams' had left the D.C. area and were living on Amelia Island at this time. All systems were go!

So in July, 1983, Cynda and I flew to Barbados where we stayed a couple of nights at Sam Lord's Castle. We had our own little cabana jutting out from the main hotel. It was perched on a thirty foot cliff overlooking a gorgeous aqua bay with steps leading down to the sparkling white sandy beach. From there we took an island hopper that carried 12 passengers and flew into Union Island. The Adams' had their yacht moored in the bay and were waiting for us. Being a pilot I have to mention, the landing strip on this island ran right up to the water's edge. The pilot had a rather high volcanic peak to go over before his flare-out to land. It gave the passengers a brief gulp and even got my attention.

The Adams' had a Caribbean Sailing Yacht (CSY) Captain on board named 'Slammer'; he was from the islands and spoke clipped English. He was about 6'5", a one-man crew and could handle most of the CSY yachts by himself. He only stayed three days and then, the Adams' were left with the Thomas'. Both Wyn and Dick were Coast Guard Captains. But Cynda and I were totally uninformed about sailing and even though I had spent some time on a smaller yacht with Mike Kennedy, I was not ready for the job at hand. However, before the eight days were over I got pretty good at crewing; and Cynda was able to steer with the rail over to the water.

From Union Island, we sailed to Petit St.Vincent, and anchored there for the night. Upon awakening the next morning, we found a French yacht had come in during the night and they were very casual with their nudity. I didn't mind at all since the gal was quite a looker, but Cynda was upset that the men were nude and extremely rude.

We sailed into the Tobago Cays and went snorkeling; the beauty of these coral islands was the underwater scenery, the exotic fish and lush colored coral reefs. There were schools of tropical rainbow fish that darted here and there. Then your eyes would spy some exceptional sea life or plant of every color swaying in these pristine clear waters. One would become so mesmerized watching the vast display that the surf could wash you out to sea without you knowing it.

From there we put into the Isle of Mustique where we explored the English Princess's Cotton House Estate on the mountain top. That evening we celebrated Dick Adams' birthday at a restaurant built out over the water and had Bananas Flambé for desert. Then it was on to Bequia where they rendered whales. It was here that this great English yacht put into the Admiralty Bay. As it slid silently along side of us, my eyes found the most beautiful sight as these two luscious Tahitian beauties stood at the rail…topless and poised like pictures on a post card. They moored not too far from our yacht and gave us all a nice show as the girls proceeded to each get a jet ski from their ship and bounce over the waves as they chased each other around the harbor. The only man we saw on board was older and had grey hair, the rest of the men were definitely crew. Must be tough to have to live like that!

Well our eight days of beautiful aqua waters and lush vegetation were almost over. The Adams' kept their CSY cutter docked at the St. Vincent Caribbean Yacht Club, and that was our last stop, from there it was back to the U.S.A. This had been a voyage Cynda and I would never forget.

◆   ◆   ◆

We finished the Tacit Blue program in 1986. Complete disappointment, humiliation, disrespect, rudeness and people insulting my intelligence and integrity started almost immediately. Reflecting back, I guess I played the game the best I could for the next fifteen years. It was a very demoralizing and depressing time. I learned to waste time by studying law; I had an office and access to a secretary, but nothing to do. Northrop couldn't think of anything to do with me, even though I was only 56 at the time. Since I was no longer flying…I must be worthless. I had so much experience and knowledge they could use, but they had people who didn't want to appear less knowledgeable. So I was not promoted to a position that might pose a threat to any superiors. They put me in a position of consultant to the B-2 group.

CHAPTER 15

THE KILLING FIELD, NORTHROP, PARKINSONS & CANCER

✦

You know how it feels when you have done your damnedest to perform a task, and then have someone kick your guts in after a great job was done. Well, this was how I was rewarded for a stupendous job on Tacit Blue by that wonderful management at Northrop. I never knew how the addlebrained hierarchy could come up with all the excuses and abuses to tear apart a good loyal employee and destroy his worth. It seemed the new management was bent on hiring and promoting incompetent junior employees and getting rid of their knowledgeable and well seasoned men.

Remember the 'accidental spin'? This story tells the vicious chaos I was put through during the Tacit Blue era. I was called back to Edwards to do the high angle of attack testing on the F-5F Saudi Airplane. Just before this call, I must set the scene right to explain what was happening at dear 'ole Northrop.

The powers that be put their two little pinheads together and came up with a plan to put the Chief Test Pilot/Manager of Flight Test Chouteau aside and put a production pilot at Palmdale in his managerial position. This particular pilot did not have an aerodynamic degree but was actually degreed in architecture! His skills were in production flying but he was 'nice' to the engineer in charge. Okay, have you got the picture?

Although I was working on a top secret project out of the area, my assignment was out of Edwards as far as Northrop was concerned. Therefore, I would be taking 'orders' or reporting to a person for whom I had little respect. Unfortunately, for me to find this out at this critical time, distressed me so that I really lost my cool and told the SOB's in charge that I refused to report to him. It seemed like an impossible situation and in reality it was, since I was on a highly classified program that he could not even comprehend including my time constraints.

Because of my new responsibilities on the secret project, it probably would have been impossible for me to have been assigned to Hank's job. Why they changed managers at this particular time was any fool's guess. Chouteau was in good health and was still capable of doing his job. His knowledge far exceeded his replacement and he was a careful boss who made sure the 'engineers' didn't kill anyone. He was not an incompetent 'yes' man.

Two new pilots came on board to fly the F-5. The pressure was put on me to show one pilot the routine for the spin program. However, in my own mind, I was so disgusted by their threats and being pulled off my secret project that I could not and would not let myself be bullied. This new pilot was in tune with the new manager and made very harmful remarks about me to the engineers who had put him there. I was threatened by a 'looney vice president', that if I did not do these AOA spin tests and report to this new manager, I would no longer be a test pilot for Northrop.

Now we are talking life and death type of testing on this airplane and I am to do these tests with this threat hanging over my head and report back to my 'new boss'. In fact, that boss killed himself in 1984 in the first F-20; and five months later the saga continued with another test pilot killed in the second F-20 practicing for the Paris air show. Both were classified as pilot errors. Both were the result of incompetent management with torpid judgment. The new F-20, the Northrop engineers were so proud of, died a rather embarrassing quiet death. This all happened in a relatively short time and was predicted early on by Thomas and Chouteau, after the promotions of inexperienced pilots by credulous 'pink' engineers calling the shots.

Another weird accident happened shortly thereafter, as the ex-chief test pilot for Northrop took it upon himself to fly a turboprop built by Brazil's Embraer. An unusual circumstance as Northrop and Embraer were under joint control and this pilot had quit his job with Northrop the day before. He allowed a Northrop test pilot friend's 17-year old son to accompany him in the second seat, during this flight something happened and the young man was ejected from the parachute equipped rear seat and landed in the Mojave Desert with mild injuries. After a thorough investigation, a highly respected person involved with the aerospace industry said the incident must have been the results of 'a very serious error in judgment'. No kidding!

Finally the 'light dawned' why I had been chosen for the secret project by Steve Smith… for some people would have objected as to my ability to do the job. The program originally was considered by some, that because they were not involved, it was going nowhere anyway and they wanted to get rid of me. Without knowing how involved this type of secret project was, and hearing bits and pieces they assumed it would be a failure and those involved would be finished. So after the project went full circle and became a glowing success, precisely because of me. Their light dimmed and they were retired. The system, however didn't change as others who took their places were inclined to play the same game. It appeared to be their corporate political exercise.

Years later, during my Parkinson's difficulty, my wife and granddaughter were pushing me in a wheelchair through WalMart in Palmdale, when we were stopped by a gentleman who apparently worked for Northrop. He didn't introduce himself but asked Alexandra, my ten-year-old grandchild, if she knew just how important her grandpa was to Northrop? Of course, she answered she did, even though I'm sure she didn't realize what he was leading up to. Then he turned to Cynda and commented what a great service I had done for Northrop Corporation. His appreciation and adulation for my work as a test pilot continued and at one point he commented to my wife regarding her speech on my behalf at the Walk of Honor banquet. He said, 'it was beautiful' and at that point he slightly choked up. Cynda asked his name and what his position was at Northrop, but all he answered was 'John' adding, 'it wasn't important. But, that Dick had done more for Northrop than any other test pilot he ever heard of or could remember'. Who knows, maybe he hadn't been there long enough to know many.

The kudos Northrop got over and over on the Tacit Blue Program were almost off the chart, especially coming from the Air Force. And I have to recognize the Northrop team that worked on Tacit Blue. They were all hand picked from seasoned employees of the best caliber. Those guys were so dedicated to their work and the project that I doubt there will ever be another group to perform as cohesively. Did they get rewarded??? Yeh, they got rewarded with a golden handshake and a kick in the pants. They tried every conceivable way to get rid of me too. But I wasn't ready to retire and I made up my mind they weren't going to make me go. So they decided no matter what I did or said they would make my life a living hell. Well, at that they were a fairly good success.

I was always trained to take notes on situations and I will refer back to some notes taken with this next episode. After Tacit Blue was finished and the B-2 was starting production, I was asked to work with the engineers in an advisory position. Then in approximately September of 1988, I was made the Manager of Flight Test Engineering. There were several engineers working on the B-2 at the time. Time schedules were always important with the Air Force and since we had been so accountable with the Air Force on our Tacit Blue Project, I believed it was equally important with the B-2 schedule. Consequently, I was disappointed to see that there was this slack attitude going on with some of the 'good ole boys club' engineers, I deemed it my job to find out the cause.

During the next two or three weeks after starting the job, I was constantly checking on certain people and jobs to see if they were, in fact, doing their job. Here is what I found. I would come home from the day shift, eat and go to bed, set the alarm for 11 p.m. get up dress and go into the plant. This is what I would find, guys on the second shift, asleep on the job or messing around drinking coffee and not doing their work. In fact, I would be so upset when I got home at 3:00 a.m.; I would sometimes wake Cynda up accidentally from tossing and turning, unable to sleep. It was so frustrating to see the irresponsibility and carelessness actually flaunted in my face. These 'engineers' didn't like to have someone who would take them to task or call them up for their actions.

Here is what happened in December, 1988, (I'll call him) 'Lain' tells me what a good job I am doing and passes this on to Roy… he agrees. Then Roy commented to me about doing such a good job; and he knew I was doing it under very adverse conditions. Good, at least they realized I was giving it my best shot…I thought.

During the second week of January, 1989, Seeless gives me the information that he is getting complaints and feedback from the engineers and suggests I have a meeting with them. He has the audacity to suggest to me that I take the approach that I am just a *poor test pilot* and humble myself asking for their support. I kept from knocking him on his ass as he so deserved; and decided not to 'eat crow'. Instead, I put together a survey in preparation for the meeting. I only got one reply after a week.

January 22, Seeless tells Balstrum at 7:30 a.m. that Dick is being removed from the Flight Test Engineering Manager position. Balstrum tells me at noon and at 1:30 p.m., Seeless tells me the same thing. Then on January 30, I inform the engineers that I am being replaced. January 31, I call another meeting and invite Seeless to assure their royal highnesses I am in charge until replaced. Seeless shows up at my meeting and informs me that Hareless is my replacement. This he does at my meeting of engineers and I have to say right here, I had never been so insulted! What a bastard…

I decided, right then and there; let the fools have their fun. The Northrop I had worked for in the 'black world' no longer existed. I would stay on and build my retirement and do whatever I wanted to do for the rest of the time I spent in their company.

February 18, Seeless gives me a letter stating that I will be reclassified and downgraded because the job I returned to in Flight Test Operations will not justify a manager position. The letter states this will happen 29 April 1989. March 9, Balstrum signs my annual review and gets threatened by Seeless and Lain for rating me good. Then there is no further action until May 26 when Balstrum is told to sign the PCR. June 14, I am given the PCR to sign implementing the change which was to happen 29 April 1989. June 15, I receive a rewritten annual review which deletes any 'good job' reference to my having ever been assigned as the Manager of Flight Test Engineering. *This is how Northrop treats their hero test pilots.* And I might add, these sneaky snake bastards are still at it I am told. I wasn't their only victim; there is a whole list of guys that had dirty poop piled on their heads.

When Welko Gasich hired me into Northrop in 1963, he paid me a great compliment; I was hired in at the top of the labor grade for test pilots. I seem to remember something Welko said when he hired me; at the time he was the Vice President and General Manager of Northrop. He told me, "Dick, one of your jobs as a Test Pilot is to hold their feet to the fire and make those engineers perform."

I never was promoted out of that labor grade, but was demotted for the outstanding job I did on Tacit Blue for the company. Welko Gasich had retired a few years prior to the Tacit Blue project.

My wife, Cynda and Bettie Ann Chouteau, hated the company so much, they used to call Northrop some of the worst names I ever heard come out of their mouths. Northrop treated Hank about the same way they treated me. I never could understand why test pilots were treated so badly at Northrop, other companies like Boeing, McDonald-Douglas, and North American really promoted their test pilots into managerial positions and vice presidents. They used their in-cockpit experience as an extension of their college credentials. Most of those guys I knew were a definite asset to their companies. But for Northrop, they hired a guy, used him up as much as they could, maybe kill him and if not, got rid of him. I have to say right here, that there were several VP's who had their heads and hearts in the right place. Those who had my back were Welko Gasich, Steve Smith, Bob Wulf, and Joe Gallagher, they were part of the real stuff that made Jack Northrop's company a success.

Then there was the new Machiavellian logic called the secondary extension, or to put it plainly, the view that politics is amoral and that any means however unscrupulous can justifiably be used to achieve power. This was their means of manipulating people remotely and in corporations often referred to as the 'backside network', where inputs are innocuously planted to produce a response from an authoritative office which will create a negative response in the target individual. But, the perpetrator continues on a friendly plane with the target… just plain back-stabbing SOB's.

First, I no longer subscribe to the 'poor me test pilot' theory. Once you have accepted the fact that corporate life is a group of predators each watching the other and covering their 'six- 0'clock' more tightly than a fighter pilot in an area faced with sup core numbers. It's the same damn dog fight! We are talking quest for power…kill or be killed!

The wanna-be test pilots are always talking about the high road, knowledge, honesty, and integrity. They believe in a quality product but not all their talent being wasted. The clan of the test pilot has diminished in stature not because corporate America has shoved them down but because they have lost their "balls". How's that for an opinion!

The profession has become saturated with wimps who are afraid of their own shadow. In the 50's, these wimps would have self eliminated in a crash resulting from their own inadequate knowledge and ability. Although the same goes today and, this has proven itself over and over when pilots are killed because of pilot error. Many times, chief pilots were selected not on their ability, but because they were 'yes' men to the engineers trying to sell their ideas to upper management. It isn't unusual to see test pilots who were superb pilots with enough self-confidence to walk out of a company, if they were treated poorly.

However having an attitude of self admiration could result in a fatal accident if the individual pilot was really not that good, especially those killed in air shows. Thinking they are the 'cream of the crop' does not allow pilots to analyze those things that do not occur as planned. Sometimes this happens when a 'blue ribbon committee of engineers' picks the pilot. What would most of those guys know, as the only time they were upside down was when they *fell out of their swivel chairs!*

The truth being *engineering* had eliminated anyone in Flight Operations who was willing to call 'a spade, a spade' and it would reflect on the safety of the flight test programs. In fact the fourteen years that Hank Chouteau was Chief Pilot, he at least held the operation together without anyone getting killed.

There are many 'old school' pilots who come to mind that did not sell out to management and made great strides in the corporate field. Now days when a pilot progresses into a higher level, there is a good chance he will not represent the pilots the way we all talk about. Why? Because he will continue to use the approach which got him promoted. There I sat for ten years building up retirement when I should have walked after I could no longer test airplanes. But, it is absurd to go back and chastise oneself for the past.

◆   ◆   ◆

Parkinson's Disease

In 1994, I was driving to San Diego in Cynda's new Cadillac when she noticed the car slightly jerking. It had very sensitive touch with the steering. Upon observation, she questioned me as to why my left hand was jerking the steering wheel. I couldn't explain it to her, and I told her I had noticed it trembling or shaking for a while. Right away she got upset and said that she was going to make an appointment with the doctor for me to have a physical. I tried to put her off and felt it wasn't necessary, but she was not to be quieted and so we made the appointment with the UCLA Medical Center's Parkinson Department. After the examination, word came back that the doctor suspected I had Parkinson's disease, but it was really too early to be sure.

I continued to work, but I realized that I was not as sharp as I had been and that my hearing was not good at meetings, leaving me feeling even more inadequate. I took the approach that I would not reply in depth to anything as I wasn't quite sure what the engineers were asking me because of my hearing problem. Cynda again got me to a doctor and I was fitted with a new hearing aid. Unfortunately, it never seemed to work very well and finally, I refused to wear it. I realized I was not being included into the stream of things anymore, but Northrop couldn't make me retire because of *who* I was and *what* I had done for the company.

In May of 1996, I came home on a Friday evening and announced to Cynda that, President Clinton had declassified the project I had worked on and it would be announced the next day on the news. Well, that night on TV a picture was shown of Tacit Blue, but very little was told about the program. There would be many new revelations at Northrop on the following Monday. People who had made derogatory remarks about 'that old man roaming around' now knew who he was and what he had done. Things changed and at last, there was respect in their eyes when they spoke to me and I began to rethink my career.

Soon a new world of notability and popularity followed me wherever I went at Northrop. The local newspaper ran their front page headlines in bold letters as 'LOCAL TEST PILOT BREAKS SILENCE'. This notoriety would continue for the next several years. So after all, I did get my 15 minutes of fame. This was the beginning of a whirlwind of recognition worldwide, starting in Dayton, Ohio on May 22, 1996.

That same year, my condition worsened as my Parkinson's symptoms became more obvious. Again, Cynda took me to the Parkinson's Center in Valencia for diagnosis. This time the doctor said I definitely had Parkinson's disease. He thought I had about five good years. It upset Cynda terribly and she was so angry at him for telling us. As this disease progressed, I realized I would not have a good chance to do anything at Northrop, but I continued to show up for work and Northrop continued to allow it. There was a lot of talk about me retiring but I was determined to stay as long as I could manage. The limelight of the Tacit Blue had not faded and I was still a focal figure strolling through the halls. Also, my only job was to stroke the guys who made vice president from the project, and I was happy to do that. They had pulled out a lot of stops to do things for me.

In 1997, my brother had been diagnosed with prostate cancer and I was concerned for him. Then in 1998 I was diagnosed with prostate cancer. After several months of going from doctor to doctor, trying to figure out the best treatment, Cynda and I decided on the pellet treatment.

We had close friends living in Encinitas, CA. This was R/ADM (ret.) Smoke Wilson and his wife, the retired admiral and I had gone to Test Pilot School at Patuxent River. Connie was a volunteer at Scripps Hospital. After researching the matter, she came up with a doctor who performed a new operation for prostate cancer. He injected radio-active isotope pellets into the cancer, and the patient would go into the hospital early morning and come out about 4 p.m. in the afternoon. There would be very little radiation sickness and minimum pain. So in September, 1998, the deed was done.

We weathered the pellets and then I was sent to a bladder specialist who discovered a lesion in the bladder and did that little laser operation right in his office. From there, the Parkinson's disease seemed to accelerate because of the radiation treatment and laser surgery. The doctors' told me anytime the body is attacked by another illness, Parkinson's will be affected. This time there was no way but to continue holding onto the existing routine until I could retire. Two weeks later, I was informed of my retirement and in October, the real friends that I had had at Northrop threw a retirement party for me. I wasn't totally up to par; the radiation hadn't made me too sick but left me feeling a little ill.

Mike Kennedy and I had established a real friendship over the years. I spoke about his boat earlier. He was still a member of the Cabrillo Yacht Club. When Mike heard about my possible retirement, he organized a grand retirement party for me at his Yacht Club in San Pedro. This was about the nicest thing anyone had ever done for me and I was in for a great treat. This was to say goodbye to my *real* friends from the old Northrop, people who I worked with and respected through the years.

Shortly after my retirement party in 1998, Cynda was advised that Northrop had agreed to put me on a two year sick leave which would keep my insurance active and give me six months of regular pay along with a graduated pay check kicking in after six months. Thanks go to the action of a super B-2 Chief Pilot and friend, Don Weiss. He was instrumental in getting the company to do this one final great gesture for me. Finally, Northrop retired me in November, 2000, at the age of 70. But the party was another story, as friends 'fried' me unmercifully.

CHAPTER 16

TACIT BLUE ROLLOUT,
KINCHLOE AWARD, & HONORS

✦

As I remarked before, in May, 1996, President Clinton declassified part of Tacit Blue and it couldn't have come at a better time. Cynda always said it was the only good thing he ever did. On a Friday night, I came home from work and announced that the secret project I had worked on was going to be declassified the next day. And, that night a picture of Tacit Blue was all over the television networks, as the highly secret stealth test bed which led to the development of the B-2 Bomber.

Then on that glorious day in 1996 at Dayton, Ohio, as those huge hangar doors began to roll back; this strange grey object slowly emerged out of the black into the sunlight. All eyes were wide with wonder, and then slowly voices began to be heard from the noise of the crowd of watchers, words about just how weird this flying *whale* really looked.

ROLLOUT AT DAYTON

Cynda's remarks were frank, as she quipped something like "That is the ugliest thing I have ever seen. Why did they make it look like that?"

Those were questions that would eventually be answered, but not at this juncture. During the next few days, we were inundated with calls and congratulations as the newspapers and word spread around the Antelope Valley. Then an invitation came for us to attend a National Air Force Roll-out at Dayton's Wright-Patterson Air Force Museum on May 22, 1996. It was Cynda's first opinion that the Air Force would not give me any recognition since I was a civilian and they had several Air Force pilots that had also flown the plane. But, she would be the first one to tell you that we both were pleasantly surprised as I got more than my share of attention and glory the day of the rollout. This next picture shows the full view of the Tacit Blue on the tarmac at Wright-Patterson Air Force Museum. It is still one of the most sought after planes to view at the museum. Where are the engines? Guess!

TACIT BLUE, 'THE WHALE'

Upon our arrival at the Wright Patterson Air Force Museum, we were taken to the secret hangar where Tacit Blue was parked. I was allowed to crawl up into the cockpit and sit in the pilot's seat again. What a thrill, I hadn't realized what an integral part 'this ole gal' had played in my life.

Cynda was allowed to crawl up into the cockpit halfway; she took the following picture of me while standing on the steps of the hatch. The hatch was in the bottom of the airplane and pulled down to open, it was quite small and a very tight fit for anyone in a flight suit. The last crew that had prepared the Tacit Blue for the museum had installed an engraved plate with the pilots' names. It was a meaningful memorial in the 'Whale'. I was the only civilian to fly it; the other four were Air Force.

DICK BACK IN TACIT BLUE COCKPIT, TAKEN BY CYNDA

To quote the generals that were in charge, rave statements were printed such as: "The Air Force hit a home run in media coverage as a result of the *TACIT BLUE* unveiling. Evidence to that fact includes ABC's World News Tonight broadcast which remarked: '*THIS ONE OF A KIND AIRPLANE WAS PART OF A REVOLUTION IN TECHNOLOGY THAT HELPED TO CHANGE FOREVER THE WAY MILITARY AIRCRAFT ARE DESIGNED.*'

Millions of viewers watched that report and similar coverage on CNN and CBS." It continued on with: "Print coverage was equally encouraging as noted in the Associated Press wire service stories which commented on the … *PIONEERING RADAR-EVADING DESIGN WHICH LIVES ON IN TODAY'S B-2 STEALTH BOMBER.*"

The next quote that was repeated around Northrop was *"NO TACIT BLUE, NO B-2"*. That came from all who worked and loved the project they had so fervently and faithfully devoted their time to.

FINALLY, CYNDA COULD BE INCLUDED IN THE PICTURE

The trip to Dayton was quite an eye-opener for Northrop, the Air Force was ecstatic with the success of this program. After the trip to Dayton, my self esteem began to resurface and I had to rethink my career. Although, I was not happy with Northrop, at least the company had provided me with an opportunity to reconcile myself to the fact that… *I had not failed,* after all!

During the next several months, Northrop held several sessions of autograph signings at the main cafeterias in Palmdale and Hawthorne. Those employees were earnestly eager to see who the old guy was and find out exactly what he did. The Northrop Public Relations team had been at Wright-Patterson and had interviewed me there on video. They also tried to interview Cynda, but she was very hesitant and after finally agreeing to be interviewed, broke down during the session and had to be excused. I had no idea that this whole thing had been such an emotional roller coaster for her. The video lighting was so poor, it made me look like a ghost and they scrapped most of it.

There were a couple of vice presidents that were my supporters. Steve Smith and Bob Wulf had believed in me from the beginning. Bob Wulf and his wife Cathy had often been our guests at the annual Society of Experimental Test Pilots banquet at the Beverly Hilton Hotel in Beverly Hills. Bob took it upon himself to nominate me for the coveted test pilot award, the Kincheloe Award. After several attempts to discourage Bob, the people running the Society finally gave in and agreed to present me with the award, but only after including the Air Force pilot that flew the first Air Force flight (which was actually the fifth flight). No matter which way the wind blows, politics will always win out.

The SETP symposium was held annually, in September, at the Beverly Hilton Hotel. Since the Tacit Blue airplane was on every pilot's lips, the Tacit Blue pilots were invited to speak at the symposium day session. Everyone was interested in hearing about this new declassified airplane. After this session was over, Cynda and I were walking down the hall with this huge group of guys that had attended when we overheard a couple of commercial pilots talking. This particular airline pilot was telling the other one his commercial route took him near the desert area where this craft was flown, probably Area 51. And as we listened, he told them he had seen the strangest looking thing flying at about 18,000 ft altitude, it had a hole in the top and seemed to be stationary, so he officially reported seeing a UFO and that was in late 1982. As he continued on, he said he was sure that it was the Tacit Blue flying. Shortly, we came to the end of the hall and when he turned and saw me, he came over to shake my hand and introduce himself. I had a little chuckle underneath it all and more secrets under my belt too.

And so, a couple of nights later, at the formal banquet, I was the recipient of this prestigious award. In my mind, I knew I had finally made it. Whatever happened from then on, the pinnacle of my career had been crowned by the most significant symbol in aerospace. To say Cynda was ecstatic along with me and a few other great friends would be an understatement.

DICK RECEIVING THE KINCHELOE AWARD AT THE BANQUET

For those of you who are not familiar with the award, let me explain what it is all about.

Because of the secrecy of his test program, this award could not be given at the time of the actual flying (First flight February 5, 1982) and was given retroactive after President Clinton declassified the project in 1996.

I knew I had been nominated for the award after the declassification, but I wasn't sure I would win. The scene was set with several Northrop co-workers seated at our table. All had been invited by Northrop. The Kincheloe award was always the last thing on the program to be presented. And I began to feel certain I had won when the overhead projected a picture of Tacit Blue on the giant screens in each corner of the room. Cynda and our daughter Velvet were experiencing tears of joy when my name was announced. We were thrilled I had been selected and as I went to the podium to receive my award, I tried to be brief and only said, "Thanks, some may deserve it more, but none would appreciate it as much, thanks to those who contributed to a successful program."

Immediately after the banquet, a huge room had been reserved by Northrop for a celebration in my honor. They had gone all out with banners and champagne, the works. It was one of those times I felt really appreciated by Northrop, and of course that group always took care of my back. This picture is with Bob Wulf, one of the Vice Presidents who nominated me.

This picture is with Max Stanley, Northrop's original flying wing test pilot and me.

The Kincheloe Award was named for Ivan Kincheloe, who was killed testing an F-104 in the early days at Edwards Air Force Base. It is the award given to the test pilot of the year for outstanding professional accomplishment in flight testing an airplane. It is the peak of recognition in the test pilot's world, and compares to the Academy Awards for actors in Hollywood.

Those early years of the SETP banquets brought out famous names like Bob Hope in the 60's, Charles Lindbergh in the 70's, David Hartman in the later years, and many more that included Hollywood's royalty. You never knew who might be sitting at the next table in that immense ballroom of the Beverly Hilton Hotel. Attendance grew through the years to about 1500 dignitaries and aerospace people.

I remember well the year Bob Hope was our Master of Ceremonies. Those years took on a relaxed atmosphere and a relief from the pressure to keep performing for your company. The fellowship of the society was more of camaraderie than politics, but those wonderful social activities were not to last. When companies started serving free booze and giving gifts to the military, things started getting out of line. Politics took over and contracts were breached for favors or promises of jobs to come after military retirement. Then restrictions were made and the individual companies could no longer have 'hospitality suites' or give military personnel gratuities. So now today there is little socializing between company representatives, only 'spies' pretending to be friendly.

The year Charles Lindberg attended the banquet was another 'dressing down' you might say. Mr. Lindberg was a choice candidate to have as speaker at our banquet, but his personality appeared restricted to extreme conservatism. As we came into the banquet hall there in the Hilton, our table was only three tables away from the Lindberg table. Before everyone was seated and the program had started, Cynda took our program and approached the Lindberg table. When she asked him for his autograph, he sharply remarked he did not sign autographs! She came back to our table feeling very chastised and embarrassed.

When Lindberg came to the podium and began to speak, his tone of voice alerted the crowd about his feelings of disgust and disapproval for everyone in the room. Cynda wasn't the only one who bore his wrath that evening, as he spoke; he attacked the test pilots like a father after his unbridled son! He told us how ashamed he was, that we were drunkards ruining the environment, not upholding our constitutional rights as good citizens. He went on and on lambasting us about being a bunch of asses with firecrackers; he told us all where to get off about being arrogant and not conserving our country until the look on our faces was of sober pallor. We were outraged underneath and quietly subdued. He had not recognized one good thing we had accomplished and threw a 'wet blanket' on our celebration…but not for long!

In the aftermath of his speech, he fanned a flame of anger from those pilots' who had put their lives on the line many times to find the 'right stuff'. After all we had brought the good old U.S.A. to the pinnacle of *LEADER in the WORLD* when it came to technology and aerospace. These guys had earned every ounce of respect and Mr. Lindbergh was 'off-the-wall and out-of-date'. Sure there were a few who got a little out of hand and jumped in the pool with their clothes on or did other ridiculous things, but all in all much had been accomplished during the business and technical sessions. Companies from around the world learned new techniques to help save lives in commercial airplanes as well as military.

The Society of Experimental Test Pilots (SETP) was an elite group of test pilots who organized in 1955. Their vision: "To be the recognized world leader in promoting safety, communication and education in the design & flight test of aerospace vehicles and their related systems. And to maintain a viable professional and prestigious international society for all test pilots and aerospace corporations."

Their mission statement: "To broaden professional relationships through the sharing of ideas and experiences which promote and enhance safety, communication and education. To prevent accidents and loss of life by improving safety, design and flight test of aerospace vehicles and their related systems. To provide a forum to disseminate information to those in the aerospace industry for the benefit of all aviation users."

My first experience with SETP came in 1963 after I joined the group. The Beverly Hilton always reserved two complete floors for the test pilots and their wives. They tried to keep them on those floors because it was two nights of all night partying and drinking. Hospitality suites were set up by all the major aerospace companies. It was a camaraderie to end all camaraderie's! The men loved what they were doing and the women loved them for who they were. Here was life being lived for today, for tomorrow it might end.

The SETP became the wives household subject of conversation and object of affection in more ways than one. The social activities during the year included meetings and elections taking place, papers for their husbands to give and of course the most important part was the culmination of the banquet at the Beverly Hilton. All of these things included the wives. Friends met from far off countries each year reviving their acquaintances and the wives were active in building relationships with other women who came from across the United States and foreign countries.

Excitement started building each year as it came time for the annual SETP banquet held at the Beverly Hilton Hotel. We would stay there at the Hilton for the entire session. This included Thursday and Friday's technical sessions, luncheons with speakers, and the Friday night pool side cocktail party. Then afterward the hosted corporate hospitality suites, that stayed open till dawn, and sometimes served breakfast style snacks.

It was one of those evening cocktail occasions I remember. Cynda and I were in Don Bowen's (TPS classmate) Sunstrand hospitality suite, and the place was packed. Everyone dressed in formal gear including the military. I was standing at the bar talking to a friend when a young stud-type military pilot asked me who that little gal was standing in the middle of a group talking. It just happened to be my wife, Cynda. He looked a little taken back and then asked me if I was a good sport. He then proceeded to tell me what he wanted to do. Now a few of us were in on the joke and we sort of sauntered into the crowd, and I introduced him to Cynda. After a few casual words of conversation he asked Cynda, "Do you know how a Pollack pulls up his socks?"

She had a little suspicious grin on her face as if she knew something was up, but answered, "No, I don't".

He immediately dropped his pants in front of Cynda, pulled up his socks, then pulled his pants back up. She burst out laughing along with the rest of the gang in the suite. She told the group later she wished she had thought of saying 'Oh, I see you've changed your underwear'. That joke kept the party going till wee hours in the morning, still laughing at the expression on Cynda's face. These were the years that one misses so much; this society of guys is not the same.

I felt overwhelmed by the vast coverage and world recognition that the society had already received. Corporations and their pilots from every corner of the universe were represented at the annual banquet held in the Beverly Hilton Hotel. I became a Fellow in the Society in 1982; this significance is the highest level of membership one can receive in the Society. And now as I look back on the last forty years of membership in the Society of Experimental Test Pilots, I feel like my fellow test pilots were an outstanding bunch of American citizens who loved to be challenged and were glad to step up to the plate. Why else would any person put his life in harms way day after day?

So SETP banquets came and went, years of friendships, deaths, divorces and remarriages to different partners. It seemed to have a life all of its' own. As the faces changed with time so did the friendships and the camaraderie…friendly faces were fewer, hospitality suites were no longer available. Military personnel were more and more in control. Aerospace was being 'governmentized' and companies were merging into giants and competition had turned into an all out war.

As I said before, life never stays the same, so be glad for having had 'the time of your life'!

◆   ◆   ◆

AIR FORCE ART PRESENTATION

Shortly after the Tacit Blue project was declassified and the roll out in Dayton had occurred. I was contacted by an Air Force artist named Jim Conahan. Jim had introduced himself to me at the Dayton unveiling. He was pursuing me to get permission to create a piece of artwork for the semi-annual Air Force Art Presentation. So for the next few months, we sent pictures and information from our files to Jim. He chose several things to put in the montage of my flying career, they included the B-52, me in my high altitude G-suit, the F-5, my No. 13 parachute that was used over the Mt. Whitney ejection, and the crowning project, the Tacit Blue Test Bed Airplane.

On October 17, 1997, Cynda and I attended the Air Force Art Presentation Banquet at the Andrews Air Force Base, Maryland. We were in for a very pleasant evening renewing some old acquaintances and meeting new ones. During the conversation at our table, Jim introduced us to the military dignitaries. When Jim explained who I was, a colonel across the table who knew about Tacit Blue made a comment of 'Oh sure' then laughed. Red faced, Jim reiterated that Dick was, in fact, the Chief Test Pilot of Tacit Blue. The colonel then jumped to his feet and grabbed my hand and became overly animated. I think he was embarrassed. Anyway, I let it go and laughed with him. From that point on, I was swamped with questions from around the table and told many stories of my career.

CYNDA AND I BY THE PAINTING DEPICTING MY FLYING CAREER

That evening was even more rewarding visiting with an acquaintance...previously the Air Force historian at Edwards AFB. Richard Hallion was the Master of Ceremonies, now the Air Force Historian in Washington D.C. During the program, he introduced me to the entire audience as an Honored Guest, and explained what I had done. I stood to be recognized and received a very warm applause from the crowd of people. There were to have been two astronauts as guests also, but neither showed up, so luckily I had the honors all to myself that night. Jim asked me to put the stories I told in a letter. So after that night I wrote the following letter to thank Jim for the wonderful expression of honor that I felt from his art work and included some of the stories I had told during dinner.

November 17, 1997

Dear Jim,

The Air Force Art Presentation dinner was an outstanding event. The many paintings depicting the flying activities gave me an emotional reaction because I had not expected to see familiar flight scenes so vividly portrayed. They expressed emotion through art which must be very difficult to achieve and which required many hours of dedicated effort.

To be the subject of your painting was a great honor, thank you. It was a memorable evening to meet the actual artists who did this work; the new Chief of Staff, General Ryan; and renew old acquaintances like Richard Hallion.

Telling stories about past 'thrills' is half the fun in flying. It was a real pleasure to exchange some of my experiences with you and the other participants at dinner, such as my ejection over the Mount Whitney area. Ejection from a fighter or any airplane that is out of control becomes a memorable event to any pilot and mine over the Sierra Nevada Mountains was no different. The flight was to check out new surveillance cameras installed in the F-5 fighter for deployment to Vietnam. After my initial run through the inverted flight maneuvers, the airplane would not stop rolling due to a jammed aileron actuator. The plane was rolling at 300 degrees per second and going straight down in an area northwest of Mt. Whitney. After quick analysis of my situation, it became evident I needed to punch out. The terrain in the area is near 14,000 feet altitude. My landing was in boulders the size of cars or larger at about 11,000 feet. The plane went straight in at about 1.2 Mach at 6000 feet!

During the early1960's Northrop was introducing the T-38's to the astronauts. NASA was planning to buy airplanes to provide flying time for them. The second group had been selected to add to the original Mercury 7 group. Another company pilot and I took our T-38 demonstrator to Houston for the astronauts evaluation. Everybody was already a test pilot, so briefings and checkouts were very limited. However, we maintained a reasonably formal approach, each pilot had all the appropriate flight equipment. The astronauts would arrive on their scheduled time and fly, however, when we reached the last flight time, that pilot had not arrived. There was no concern, because we knew the astronauts were very busy, but it was getting late.

Finally, Gordon Cooper arrived wearing a sport shirt, slacks and loafers. We briefed and politely talked until one of our people suggested the airplane was ready and would Mr. Cooper like to get his flight gear? Cooper's reply was "I'm ready".

We had taken pictures with all the astronauts by the airplane (Cooper in slacks and parachute). We had a good flight with Gordon Cooper but NASA never included a copy of our picture with him. It just shows that even a maverick could have the 'Right Stuff'.

Tacit Blue is another story very dear to my heart because good fortune allowed me to be a key player on the team and we kept it secret for over 15 years. The real high point of it all is to know that the painting will preserve the spirit of 'Tacit Blue'. Hopefully it will hang in the Air Force Museum with the airplane. There were many events in the short life of this flying program, but I think the team was most proud of the fact that we had the same plane at the end of testing as we started with, no accidents!!

The first flight was short. Tacit Blue was really new technology but because of ordinary technology we had to abort…a circuit breaker popped out at lift-off so ground control had no TM linkage and no data. On board data worked but we aborted. It was successful because on any flight, first or 100th, if you take off and land successfully… it is a success. I flew the first four flights of Tacit Blue and over 70 of the total 135 flights. There were only five pilots who flew the bird, the other four were Air Force pilots.

I will look forward to sharing more 'war stories' on Tacit Blue with you another time.

Thanks again Jim for your interest.

Sincerely,

Dick Thomas, Chief Test Pilot for Tacit Blue Project

◆   ◆   ◆

THE RETIREMENT PARTY

In 1998, my health continued to deteriorate with the Parkinsons and as I mentioned earlier in September of 1998, I was operated on for prostate cancer by the doctor implanting the radiation pellets right into the cancer. Two weeks later those rascally guys from Northrop had put together a 'Roast' in my honor at Mike's yacht club with a program by Northrop that surprised us all.

Because of the pellet implant, I didn't feel up to par as the effects of radiation had made me slightly nauseous. I prepped for the retirement party not expecting much. However, my friends at Northrop did not fail me, as my family and I were to find out very soon.

Roy Martin, my buddy test pilot acted as Master of Ceremonies. Other main speakers included Mike Kennedy (the real instigator of the party), and Steve Smith, retired Vice President who had originally selected me for the Tacit Blue program. Many others spoke each bringing a gag gift along with a barb!

Roy's opening words went something like this, "Well, this is the third annual retirement party for Dick Thomas. You know Northrop thought that guy was harder to get rid of than President Clinton. We thought we were going to have to impeach him to get rid of him!"

This brought guffaws and set the stage for the coming jokes regarding my 'life' at Northrop. Roy continued on, "When, Mike told me we were going to throw this party and asked me to MC, I scratched around to see if anyone had any dirt on Dick Thomas? Now when you are asking for dirt about Dick Thomas, you are in a target rich invironment with either total fiction or absolute truth."

"On one such occasion, it was a simple test and with Dick's crabby personality, the story went something like this. The F-5 was configured with rocket pods and Dick was to take it up and perform rotations. The test card was written with the CG about 3% aft of the limit on the airplane. And as soon as he started his rotations, he had a face full of airplane. Realizing he was not within the limits of the airplane, he called for an abort. After landing he calls the chief engineer for a debrief with the engineers. He then tells the engineers sitting across the table from him, that they are trying to kill him! And Ernie tells him, if they were trying to kill him he would already be dead."

This is a true story and I can honestly say, it wasn't the first time we pilots had to watch out for mistakes the engineers made. The 'Roast' continued on and on, and the crowd consisting of six or seven retired Vice Presidents was enjoying these hilarous jabs and puns. At this point the film crew started the film. Bill Kelly did a great job with Northrop's creative film department, as it had outtakes of real flying along with some imaginery spoofing. They depicted me landing in the forest on Mt. Whitney during deer hunting season (which is actually true and a hunter saw me eject and watched me land on the side of Mt. Whitney). However, in the film my helmet had a huge rack of antlers and I was being shot at by the hunters. If you remember my story, I did have matches and started a small brush fire, but there were no trees in the area, because I was above the tree line. But, in the film, I started a tremendous forest fire. Naturally, this got the guests attention and kept the 'Roast' roaring along.

The best spoof was when they depicted me accidentally dropping those two dead bombs in the General's 'back yard at Edwards'. Now everyone knew that I didn't actually drop them in the back yard but they had a picture of Saddam Hussein reclining on a chase lounge and the bomb coming down and hitting him right in the crotch. This sent the participants into fits of laughter. We all were really having a good time at my expense. I wouldn't have changed one thing.

There were some serious presentations too and one of those was from Erwin Aerospace Company that builds parachutes. Their representative, Tony Taylor, presented me with the company's distinctive Caterpillar lapel pin for my ejection over the High Sierras. Then Curtis Peebles the author of "Dark Eagles" presented me with his autographed book.

The stories continued for an hour or more and then Steve Smith took over again and told his story about selecting Dick to be the Chief Project Pilot on Tacit Blue. His story went something like this when he called Carl Wyle, "Hey Carl, we've got this problem with this thing, it's weird in both pitch and yaw! Who do you think could fly it?"

Carl didn't hesitate but came right back with, " I know just the guy for you, Dick Thomas. That guy can fly anything unstable!"

Dick's reputation at Edwards was certainly not glorious, but not cowardly either. So when Steve suggested the name of Dick Thomas as chief pilot for Northrop…Colonel Pete Knight was speechless and said, "I'll get back to you."

The rhetoric continued and Steve finally finished by saying, "but the engineers love this guy, he can do anything, 360 degrees pitch hang up, anything unstable in pitch and yaw!"

And, since Northrop was responsible for the airplane, Steve Smith, had the last say and Dick was his man. Then Steve called Don Weiss to the podium, and Don was the B-2 Chief Pilot at the time. His presentation was probably the most significant of any as he made his speech saying, "Dick you have made your mark on aerospace and we at Northrop think you should at least walk away with a piece of the airplane."

The Northrop T-38 rudder pedals with the Northrop logo imprinted on them were actually used in the B-2 Bomber. Don had one of those made into a trophy and engraved. And I was pleased to actually get that particular piece of momento.

Steve introduced Pete Soule, a college buddy of mine and brought him up to speak. Pete told a story of when we were both in the Air Force. Pete was stationed in Alaska and I in Seattle. So this is the tale Pete told us. "We had kept in touch and Dick decided he wanted to fly up to Alaska. So permission was given for him to make the flight in February, 1954. Now anyone who wanted to go to Alaska in February had to be out of their mind. But Dick, flew up and we had a good visit. Since the squadron in Alaska only had those nasty F-89's to fly, those pilots were scared to fly the thing. It had such a bad reputation and we already had had two accidents in a very short time. We had gone to the theatre that night and after the show, Dick wanted to go to the pilot's lounge, have a drink and make friends. Since I was not a pilot I couldn't go with him."

"Well, after a drink, Dick began to sing the following song to the tune of *TA RA RA BOOM DE YAY:*

IF YOU FLY AN EIGHTY-NINE,
YOU MUST BE DEAF, DUMB AND BLIND
YOUR LIFE AIN'T WORTH A DIME,
WHAT'S YOUR SCHEDULED BLOW-UP TIME?
A RA RA BOOM DE YAY, DID YOU GO BOOM TODAY?
TWO BLEW UP YESTERDAY, YOU'RE JUST NOT HERE TO STAY
TA RA RA BOOM DE YAY"

"The next day some of the guys asked me, 'who was that guy?' and I answered, 'I have no idea'. But I have to tell you, I met a guy from Edwards AFB once at a meeting in Los Angeles, as I worked for Raytheon. I asked him if he knew Dick

Thomas with Northrop. He said he did, and I can say I know Dick Thomas and I'm proud to know him."

After hearing that great song, it was my turn at the podium to give back some of what I had just been given! I think I did myself proud with little preparation in advance. As I started to speak, Jack Fagan interrupted me, he had made a model of Captain Nemo's deep sea diving machine, the Nautilaus. (I was often called 'Captain Nemo' out at the 'Area'.) Jack came to the podium and presented the model to me. I accepted it and he left the podium.

Quickly I corrected their charges, "I thought of all the things I could use against you in rebuttal to everything you said. Not strong charges of truth with every story…all the parts were there and pieces, and if you had put them together a little differently they could have been true. I wasn't quite sure how I was going to get you back, but I think Jack Fagan just gave me the answer. That is, if you engineers built the Tacit Blue the way you remember my stories, it sure enough would have come out looking like Captain Nemo's Nautilaus!"

"About those dead bombs, I didn't drop the bombs in the General's back yard. But one of them was retained in the sewer plant settling ponds and the other one skipped out across the dry lake bed. Months afterwards the Edwards patrol would come up to my office and unroll a big sheet of plots and have me look at this again asking just where did the other bomb go? So I finally just pointed to the middle of one of the sewer settling ponds and said I thought it was about 40 ft down and he probably should get his scuba gear and go down and find it. After that he never came back, so I guess he found it!"

The crowd continued to roar and carry on after each explanation that I had given. I continued on. "Then when I was flying the X-21 those engineers down in the belly of the plane would beg for just five minutes more until we were almost out of fuel. If I could fly the plane and make only *one* turn in three or four hours, it was considered highly successful."

" Now as I look out and see everyone of you, I know we have touched each others lives. Everyone of you has had an interface in my life. I've enjoyed it all, I'd do it again. But I have to remind the engineers, you didn't get me!"

This concluded the wonderful evening of reminescing with retired Vice Presidents Welko Gasich, Milt Kouska, Steve Smith, Joe Gallagher, Dave

Deering and Bob Myers. So many of the good 'old' Northrop people were there. Steve Smith's words were prophetic as he said, "this group will probably never be together again."

It was, in fact, our closing chapter. Looking back now, it doesn't seem as if my efforts were so futile, in fact, I feel like I might have made my mark in aerospace after all. As time passed, I was beginning to have more and more difficulty functioning. I could no longer keep my checkbook in order. Driving my car was a hazard to others as I could not always make my legs and feet work the pedals. Tremors were getting worse in my hands and sleep was difficult to accomplish. Deep down inside, I felt a sad desperation to fix it somehow, but was there really a way to do it?

CHAPTER 17

THE DISASTEROUS PALLIDOTOMY IN 2003

✦

Most of my life had been spent taking risks but I guess in my old age I was too indecisive. And I made the most unfortunate decision to let a quack doctor perform the pallidotomy on my brain in hopes of regaining my composure from the Parkinson's tremors. I wanted the procedure in order to be able to speak in front of my airplane, the Tacit Blue, at the Air Force museum.

It was 2003, the Centennial Celebration of the Wright Brothers historical first flight. A grand presentation was being prepared at the Wright-Patterson Air Force Museum. Pilots whose first flight airplanes were in the museum had been asked to speak in front of their plane, and tell their story of the first flight. What a great opportunity I thought. As I started to prepare for my speech, I realized how difficult it was for me to coordinate my thoughts and write them down. Due to the Parkinson's dementia that was setting in, it seemed I could not concentrate enough to accomplish my objective.

Three weeks before we were to leave for Dayton, Cynda took me to Dr. Iacono's for my regular check up and as we walked into his office, he announced to us his intention to do the pallidotomy operation the following week on Tuesday. Cynda argued with him stating that we were scheduled to fly to Dayton on the 30th of April and already had our plane tickets and hotel reservations. He immediately assured her that I would be much better and probably a lot clearer in my thinking if I had the operation. In fact, he told her he had already scheduled it for April 15th.

What followed was a heated conversation with the doctor. Cynda proceeded to question him regarding his success rate, and he always came up with the same answer. He claimed to have done 1500 of these operations with only a 2% risk factor. After a lengthy question and answer period, he told us to let him know yes or no by the following Friday.

During the week following, Cynda and I talked it over several times. My mind oscillated back and forth many times during the week but as I tried again to create my speech, the more I felt I needed to have the operation to be comfortable in giving it. So on Friday morning, I first told her 'no' for the operation and as she got on the phone to Iacono's office, I quickly changed my mind and told her 'yes'. Cynda was not in favor of the operation and had a gut feeling that it wasn't the best thing for me.

On the following Monday morning, we were to go to Iacono's office and receive instructions regarding the hospital. The original hospital, we thought, was the renowned Loma Linda Hospital. But on that fateful morning, we found it was to be the St. Bernadine Hospital in San Bernardino. When Cynda questioned the doctor again why that was, he made a derogatory remark regarding Loma Linda and said he liked St. Bernadine Hospital better. As we prepared to leave his office, he said he needed to take my blood pressure again. Cynda asked what it was. The nurse turned to her and replied, 175 over 114.

Cynda exclaimed, "My God, you can't do surgery on him tomorrow, he'll have a stroke!"

Iacono quickly asked, "Hey Dick how high was your blood pressure when you flew the first flight on Tacit Blue?"

I replied, "Oh, probably 250 over 150". Then we both laughed a little.

"Well, I don't think that is funny and I don't think Dick should have the operation." Cynda countered.

We left the office to go to the hospital for post-op including blood work and filling out the necessary paperwork. Instructions had been given to Cynda on which route to take to St. Bernadines; however, in her nervous frame of mind she became lost and could not find the hospital. She just kept saying, "This is a sign, and I don't think God wants us to do this."

Finally, she turned the car around and headed back to the doctor's office. She went back into his office and told them we couldn't find the hospital and she didn't think the pallidotomy was a good idea. The nurses started their sales pitch telling her how much better I would be and how everything would be just fine. They gave her clearer instructions for finding the hospital and off we went again, this time finding the place and getting all the necessary work done.

The next morning as we drove through the Cajon Pass south on the 138 Highway to San Bernardino, we encountered rain, sleet, hail and snow. Again, she said, "I think the Lord is telling us not to do this."

I made some crazy statement and acted mad at her, so on we went, towards 'the road to hell for me'. Little did I know I was signing away what quality of life I had left, to the hands of this incompetent madman.

The nightmare started about 4 p.m. as the doctor came to the pre-op room to put me on the gurney to take me to the operating room. Cynda and I had checked into the hospital about 8 a.m. that morning. Iacono had scheduled three other pallidotomies that day and I was to be his fourth.

I had slept on and off most of the day as the nurse had given me a couple of pills to relax me. I was to be awake for the operation and according to Iacono, the operation would only take about 20 minutes. As this cocky little bastard started instructing the interns to wheel me down the isle to be operated on, something in me came alive and I told him in no uncertain terms, "I've changed my mind and I don't want to do this." Then I repeated myself and tried to grab the rail along the hall with both hands to stop them.

Iacono, insisted I would be all right, but I argued with him again that I did not want to go through with this. At that point he became agitated and sternly said, "You are going to go through with this and be just fine!"

When we arrived at the operating room, they sat me upright on a table. I could hear Iacono giving instructions to his office aid, Felipe and the two nurses assisting. It was very cold in the room and with Parkinson's, getting chilled makes one tremble and shake. Consequently, I began to have severe tremors. They proceeded to try to put the wooden stereotactic headset frame over my head but it did not fit. Iacono was very short and Felipe was somewhat taller but not a lot. So it took the two of them to complete the deed. They were beginning to scare me by forcing the too-small frame over my head. Then after finally getting it down to rest on my shoulders, there were two white plastic screws at the top. The doctor had the nurses screw those into the flesh of my forehead, breaking the skin and causing blood to run down both sides of my face. At this point, I became rigid. My legs were extended stiffly in front and my arms were stretched as far as they could be on either side of my body. I could not talk even though I knew everything that was going on. My mind was working but words would not come out. I heard Iacono say to me, "Dick, what is the matter?" and then he said to his assistants, "My God, he has a big head."

It occurred to me that he had never even measured my head and I knew then I was in serious trouble. I heard him tell Felipe, he was going to go get Mrs. Thomas and he left the room and brought Cynda into the pre-operating room where I was. He asked her repeatedly what was wrong with me. She was in such a state of shock; she kept answering that she didn't know.

Then she turned to me and took hold of my feet, "My God honey, what is the matter, your feet are so cold."

Later I was to hear her tell our daughters that when she walked into the room and saw blood running down both sides of my face, all she could think of was Jesus's crucifixion! She told them there were no wires hooked up to me to monitor my blood pressure or heart rate and I know she was in a panic and stunned beyond belief.

Iacono continued on in his alarming way ordering the nurses to put the Plexiglas helmet over the wooden frame. There were four seating screws in the base of the helmet that would normally fit into the wooden frame so they could be fit properly together. However, the wooden frame had been sprung from the force of putting it over my head and the screws would not line up with the holes.

While Cynda stood there watching this horrific scene, she was appalled at the incompetence of the operation. Then Iacono yelled at the shaking nurse to get the screws tightened and when she could not do that, he yelled at Felipe to help him and they proceeded to get only three screws to seat in the frame. At this point Iacono was so frustrated he commented to Cynda, "This guy has the biggest head I have ever seen! Is he claustrophobic?"

"Are you kidding?" She answered back.

I was in my state of rigid tremors all this time. This had to be a nightmare because to go over it again simply does not seem realistic in the age we live in, but it gets worse!

Frantically, Iacono yells at Felipe to get Dick moving to the CAT scan room where the operation would take place. It was the usual panel of buttons and knobs on a console. A long glass window looked into the room where they took me. There was a huge dome like apparatus on the ceiling. As Cynda followed along, the doctor quickly asked, did she want to watch?

Her horrified answer was an astounding "No! I couldn't." Then she left and went to the waiting room, still wondering what she should do.

Shortly thereafter, I heard the loud squeal of the drill bit and felt the excruciating pain as it punched a hole in my right skull. I collapsed and became unconscious and did not know anything from that point on.

The following incidents were taken from Cynda's notes that she scribbled after this harrowing episode. She had gone to the waiting room about 4:30-4:45 p.m. and looked at her watch thinking about 20 minutes and he will be out of there feeling good. At about 5:30 p.m. she witnessed a person being pushed on a gurney past the waiting room, as she glanced up. Upon second glance, she realized it looked like me. She quickly picked up her purse and ran after the interns but they went through a door and it closed. Since she wasn't totally sure it was me, she went back to the waiting room. Finally at 6:00 p.m., wondering what was taking so long, she left the waiting room and went around to the operating room to ask about her husband and the whereabouts of the doctor?

One women nurse and one male nurse were in the little office outside the operating room. When she asked about her husband, they told her he was still in the operating room with the doctor. Again, she asked to see the doctor and they told her he would see her shortly. Strange vibes began and a sinking feeling came into the pit of her stomach. But, she returned to the waiting room again. Shortly, Iacono and his side-kick, Felipe, came to the waiting room. My clothes were in a large plastic bag that the hospital had given us; Cynda had her own carry bag with a book, besides her purse. Iacono asked if all that was ours and in the second breath told her just to leave that stuff and bring her purse.

Upon asking him where she was going, he told her he was taking her to the Surgeons' Lounge for a cup of coffee. Immediately, Cynda began to think the worst which seemed justified by all the actions that had preceded the operation. When they arrived at the lounge, Iacono ordered himself a cup of coffee and since Cynda did not drink coffee, he offered her water. Felipe brought the doctor his coffee and Cynda watched as Iacono proceeded to put three packages of sweetener into his cup and slowly stir it. As she waited for him to speak, she felt a sinking feeling come over her. Starring at him while he slowly sipped his coffee, she felt anger rise up in her throat and she had to restrain herself to keep from slapping him as he made her wait.

Finally, he cleared his throat and made a slight sigh as he said, "Well, the surgery didn't go as well as I planned. Dick collapsed when I started the operation and I continued on with the electronic probe to put a lesion in, after all I didn't want to just leave him the way he was."

Cynda sat there starring at him and asked, "Where is he now and can I see him?"

"I had to put him in Intensive Care, because he has not regained consciousness. But I will check on him in a few minutes and then I will let you know if you can see him."

"What is the prognosis?" She asked.

Instead of answering her, he told Felipe to get him another cup of coffee, which he did, and she watched as Iacono added his three packages of sugar again and stirred slowly. Then slowly he mumbled, "I'm not quite sure because he is still unconscious!"

He continued to tell her exactly what had happened after she left the CT room. He clearly stated that when he started to drill into Dick's skull, he collapsed; and since Dick was not awake to do the things he was supposed to do,

Iacono did not know exactly where to put the lesion, so he took a guess at it and might have put it on the wrong nerve!

At this point Cynda said she felt quietly hysterical, and as Iacono proceeded to order his third and fourth cups of coffee from his office aid, she decided to control her emotions and causally said, "Well doctor, do you think he will be okay? I know you were trying to help him."

It was the perfect ploy as Iacono, then came clean and admitted he might have made a mistake saying, "Well, think how I feel, I thought I had *killed him!*...it took me an hour just to get calm enough to come out and talk to you."

Cynda then demanded to see me and Iacono agreed, so they and Felipe left the surgeon's lounge and went back to the 4th floor. Iacono had me removed from the ICU and brought back to the CAT scan room to redo the brain scan. While Cynda and the doctor waited in the hall, very few words were spoken, and then finally the nurse brought me out of the room on the gurney where every dog and cat could walk by and see what was going on. Iacono hit me hard in the chest and began to yell in my face, "Dick wake up, Dick wake up!"

The doctor was panicky according to Cynda's report. Then he asked her to try and wake me, she then attempted to wake me also by touching my face and pulling my eyelids back, only to see the eyeball was rolled back into my head with only the whites of my eye showing. She cried, "Honey, please, please wake up." But I could not hear her. I was still unconscious.

Then a nurse came carrying an x-ray type negative into the hall and gave it to Iacono, he quickly grabbed it and held it to the ceiling hall light. The lighting in the hall was very poor and it is doubtful that he really saw anything, but he yelled out, "There is a God after all, I think he will be just fine."

The real truth would come out the next morning when Cynda arrived at the hospital at 8:15 a.m. When she asked for Richard Thomas, she was told I was out of ICU and on the 6th floor. As she walked into my room expecting me to look normal, she immediately came unglued and after taking one look at me realized I had had a stroke. My face sagged miserably on the left side, my left arm hung limp and I had a strange look on my face. She started crying and screamed, "Oh my God, honey what has he done to you?"

Whirling around, she ran to the desk and demanded to see Dr. Iacono. The nurse picked up the phone and paged him and in a few minutes he came strutting into my room. During the time it took for him to get there, Cynda had discovered my eyesight was greatly impaired, I could barely talk and I could not use my left arm or leg. The stage was set and the doctor was about to get his pedigree read in a very short time.

As he came into the room, Cynda began her tirade and confronted him; he quickly told her a bunch of lies hoping to bring back some hope to counteract her disappointment. He walked over to the bed, uncovered my right foot and brought his thumb nail up the bottom of my foot. I quickly jerked my foot back and he said, "See, Mrs. Thomas, he is going to be just fine."

Of course, at the time, it was my left foot that was partially paralyzed from the stroke. This crap kept up for several days, Cynda was concerned as I couldn't see, I couldn't swallow, and I couldn't function or talk very well. I was totally dehydrated from no liquid intake because I couldn't swallow. They were not giving me IV's and I couldn't eat. The doctor had given no instructions to help me and the hospital was literally starving me to death for lack of orders!

Cynda insisted they find out why I couldn't see, but the dumb bastard had put the lesion over the optical nerve and it gave me a double hemianopsia---meaning I could see out of the right half of the right eye and the right half of the left eye but they would not focus together and things were looking scrambled to me. However, if I looked to the extreme right I could see fairly well for about a space of 12 inches.

After two or three days, Cynda started looking at my chart and noticed I was only taking 300-400 calories a day. She went to the nurses station and asked what they intended to do and they told her that they had no instructions from Dr. Iacono. I was in misery and starving to death because I was unable to swallow and they were still not giving me any IV's. Then the doctor came in and told me to get up and walk. He even tried to get me to run in the hall! Cynda told the doctor again what she thought and he told her he was doing all he could. Exasperated and angry she went to the nurses' desk and asked them what to do. Surprise, they told her to get a good lawyer.

Now she finally got them to do the scope on my throat and it was decided that there was no obstruction, but the lesion Iacono had put in my brain somehow made my tongue and throat paralyzed. Maybe it was the stroke too, as it was later confirmed that I did indeed have a severe stroke at the time of the operation, even though Iacono had vehemently denied it. But anyone with an ounce of sense could see that I had all the symptoms.

Iacono denied it all along but after ten days in the hospital, he finally decided he would recommend I be put in the Ballard Rehabilitation Facility. So I was transferred to Ballard. At Ballard, Iacono's name was a 'dirty word'. Their doctors had no respect for Iacono and told us he was atypical---meaning he did not medicate to procedure but did things 'off the chart'. It was too late for us to find this out. I became weaker and weaker and was in such pain, Cynda finally asked the Ballard doctor if he was going to starve me to death? The doctor then agreed to put a G-tube into my stomach so I could get nourishment. It was done the next day, however, by this time I had lost 30 lbs. I cannot tell you the anguish and hell I went through during those next few weeks that literally became months.

During those first weeks at Ballard after the G-tube, I began to get some strength back. Cynda had been going back to the St. Bernadine Hospital to get the surgeon's report of my surgery. We could never get it as he had not made one up and it was now going on 30 days since the operation. The doctors at Ballard wanted to see my X-rays and she was able to get those so my new doctors could examine them and figure out what had happened to me. Finally, her last attempt to get the doctor's statement paid off and as she was leaving the records area with his statement, she ran square into him in the hall. There was no place for him to hide as he squirmed around trying to be nice. She was not going to accept it. She confronted him, "Well if it isn't Doctor Iacono?"

He immediately responded, "Oh Mrs. Thomas, how is Dick doing?"

"Terrible, you ought to know, you did it to him," she boldly commented.

Unfortunately, she had not read his report at the time; if she had the world would have spun out of control. As Iacono had written a completely fictitious report, all lies about how Dick was alert and awake during the entire operation! But she continued on. "He can't see, he can barely swallow and he is not able to walk yet. I suppose you hoped you would never see us again."

"Oh, I will go to Ballard and see him, he should be doing well by now, but I must be going as I have an operation to perform now," and he started to leave.

"Well, I certainly hope the guy you are going to operate on is luckier than Dick was and doesn't come out half dead!" She told him as he left the hall and hurried on to his next victim.

The following week, Iacono made an appointment with the Ballard doctors to discuss my condition and what they could do to improve my situation. Cynda made it known to the Ballard doctors that she was to be there when Iacono came to see me and talk to my new doctors. She asked an acquaintance from Northrop to come as a witness when she talked to Iacono. Bob Kaminski came to Ballard and was there with us in the room when Iacono came in to check me over and talk to Cynda about what progress I might be able to make. Bob's assessment of Iacono was the same as Cynda's basically. They both agreed he was a total ass with an over supply of *'ego'* and not enough brains to accompany his ego.

Iacono was a pilot and thinking Bob was a pilot, immediately started bragging about his own accomplishments in flying his airplane. After Iacono's meeting with the Ballard doctors, the two of them came to me and told me they refused to do what he had asked them to do; and that was give me a double supply of Prozac and Zoloft each to shock the brain. They were very skeptical about his treatment and asked Cynda if she wanted them to do that. She said no, of course. Then they looked at the x-rays and told her that I had definitely had a severe stroke during surgery.

A couple of days later when my daughter, Velvet was with me, Iacono showed up again. He was so stupid some times it was unbelievable. He insisted I get up and walk; now I had only been walking with help from a physical therapy walking guide that had rails on both sides that were about eight feet long. It was early evening and I was in a hospital gown. The weather was chilly and he insisted I go outside. I was able to get up with the help of Velvet, as Iacono was urging me to walk into the hall and go outside in my hospital gown. Velvet was so distressed, she started arguing with Iacono and said, "Why are you doing this to him, he is about to fall down and it is too cold outside?"

Iacono's reply was, "the fresh air will do him good!"

I called out to Velvet that I was falling and she grabbed me and took me back to my bed. Iacono followed us into the room and started telling Velvet how great he was at helping these Parkinson's patients. She cleaned his clock right then and there telling him, "Look, Iacono, this isn't about you, it's about my *DAD* and you need to leave your damn ego at the door when you come in here!"

That was the last time any of us saw Iacono. We tried to sue with an attorney in Westwood; he took $2000 and told us we had a good case against Iacono. But, after six months we found we only had an empty wallet. Nothing was done as no neuro-surgeon would testify against a fellow neuro-surgeon in California; even though they commented they knew Dr. Iacono was doing 'out of the box' practices. Velvet decided to complain to the California State Medical Board. After a year or so, she got a letter from them stating that "Doctor" Robert P. Iacono had lost his license and could no longer practice in California and several other states. He closed his practice and moved out of state.

My youngest daughter, Velvet, was a constant help to Cynda and especially me. I was put in some of the worst care homes and I can tell you Velvet was there to help us as much as she could be even though her teaching job was demanding of her time.

Cynda had asked friends of hers to come and pray over me asking that I would walk out of the hospital by the end of August. And on that day, I was able to walk from my room to her car. It was a long road back as I only weighed 152 lbs. I still had the G-tube in my stomach, but I had started trying to eat several weeks back and could eat soft foods and drink thickened water and milk. The food at the care home was the worst, and after Cynda got me home and started feeding me six little meals a day, I began to gain weight. The doctors all thought I would die in less than six months when they sent me home with hospital bed, hospice and all.

In six months, Cynda had me back walking even though I could not see very well. The hospital bed went back and I began sleeping in a regular bed. I had been able to eat soft foods and one night after trying to sleep with a g-tube in my gut, I got disgusted and pulled the damn thing out and threw it on the floor. Cynda wasn't feeding me through it anymore and I didn't like the feeling of that tube sticking into my stomach.

It wasn't long before I was able to go with a couple of Northrop buddies and hit golf balls. I could hit the ball about 100 yards if it was placed in front of my right foot, but I couldn't see where it went because of my 'legally blind' eyesight. It was great exercise and felt good to get out and talk to those guys I had worked with, especially Lee Phillips. Lee had been the first Quality Assurance Manager on Tacit Blue, checked everything out before the first flight, put me in the cockpit and was there for me when I landed. What a great guy!

Because of all this, Cynda and I didn't get to celebrate our 45th wedding anniversary in Hawaii as we had planned for that June. Of course, I was totally incapacitated when the Wright-Patterson Celebration took place and Cynda asked Dan Vanderhorst, who had flown Tacit Blue also, to speak for me. At least I was not in a fog all the time. I was able to review a lot of events with my daughter, Velvet. She was so interested in everything from childhood up. Those moments of clarity were very sad and I had many regrets. I knew that things were not ever going to get back to normal for me and I became very depressed. I think Cynda did her share of crying too, but the road would get harder for her as I progressed with my disease. The operation had caused my dementia to become more obvious and the neurologist here in Lancaster informed her I had Alzheimer's.

The year 2003 was the worst; at the time I was still in the 'Kevorkian' care home. Then in July, Cynda was rear-ended at the end of a long line of cars stopped for a red light near the A.V. Mall. That did about $5500 worth of damage to her Lexus. About three weeks after her wreck, Velvet left my care home to go to her condo in Newhall. A stalled car on the freeway caused her to have a wreck and break her nose and hurt her shoulder and neck.

I was finally home at the end of August and things seemed to be getting better. Cynda was taking care of me and our son, Rich, who was having depression problems and had moved home. It was now October and Cynda had her car back for about two months. She had picked up our granddaughter, Alexandra, after school to go shopping. As she came through the green light near our home, a red pickup truck ran the red light and hit her in the driver's door. Alexandra was in the back seat behind her and was not hurt, but Cynda's left arm was broken in two places and she was covered in glass from head to toe. The Lexus was totaled and after Cynda was put back together with a steel plate and seven screws in her arm, she was able to carry on with her caretaker responsibilities. It seemed we were never able to get out from under the black cloud following us.

But before I say goodbye, I must finish my story as there were some good things to come. In October, 2004, the renowned Eagles of the Flight Test Historical Society at Edwards presented me their Golden Eagle Award at their annual Gathering of Eagles Banquet. And in September, 2005, The City of Lancaster finally recognized me on their Walk of Honor.

CHAPTER 18

GATHERING OF EAGLES & WALK OF HONOR

✦

The road to success has not been an easy one and sometimes I wonder if I made the right decisions in my life. When you come to the final days and your time on this earth is short, you wonder, was it all worth it? Did I accomplish anything at all? You realize that you are just an award in some museum or a piece of paper in someone's scrapbook. In my opinion, the only way I see any success is to be measured by your constituents. So how are we measured?

When I was presented my Golden Eagle by the Edwards Flight Test Historical Society's Gathering of Eagles banquet, I realized that *they* believed I had done my job successfully. *They* were a group of test pilots and engineers from the earliest years who had made great strides in aviation, names and faces renowned for their dedication and recognized world wide.

Since my surgery in 2003, I was legally blind and could not feed myself. I was not able to see exactly where I was going and my hearing was also impaired. If you've got the picture, you know how hard it would be to function in a room full of test pilots, wives and other dignitaries. Nevertheless, Cynda, insisted on my being there and actually helped me through the whole thing. I never imagined how embarrassing it might be for her to feed me at a banquet style dinner, but she did just that and didn't seem to mind. During the presentation when it was my turn to receive my 'Golden Eagle', Roy Martin helped me to the stage and I was able to say a few words of how grateful and honored I was. This was October, 2004.

◆   ◆   ◆

Lancaster's Walk of Honor started in 1990 with prominent names anyone would recognize; A. Scott Crossfield, Gen. James Doolittle, Col. Pete Knight, Tony LeVier, and Brig. Gen. Chuck Yeager. It continued on the following years with names like Neil Armstrong, Pete Everest, Fitz Fulton, Max Stanley, Fred Haise, Bill Park, Hank Chouteau, Jesse Jacobs, and many more. Each year as I wrestled with myself, I became more and more convinced I had not made the grade as I knew that those who already had a bronze placard on the boulevard were measuring each nominee and deciding in their own mind who was worthy.

As the years started passing me by, I became apprehensive each year at the time when the Walk of Honor recipients were named. It was disappointing, as I was ignored year after year. After the declassification of Tacit Blue, I believed this evidence along with receiving the Kincheloe Award would surely give me enough limelight to get me the recognition I deserved. But it didn't happen. It wasn't until I was completely disabled that I was finally honored in 2005. At this point in my life, I was still able to understand the significance of the honor, but not able to speak or enjoy the program.

Cynda had been a fairly successful realtor in Lancaster for twenty-five years. During our early years in Lancaster, she had enjoyed volunteering with a group called the Alpha Charter Guild. She had previously worked for Lockheed in customer relations; and was not shy at meeting the public. So she took it upon herself to speak for me at the banquet.

As Cynda started preparing for her upcoming speech for the Walk of Honor, she realized it wasn't going to be easy to speak in front of all those people. There were the city dignitaries and most of aerospace 'royalty' that included many test pilots and their wives. She started researching everything she could get her hands on regarding my past programs and the engineers who worked with me on them. Lee Phillips was called to our house and as he talked, she took notes and asked question after question about Tacit Blue and other programs that Lee knew about. She contacted Bob Wulf, Vice President and Roy Martin, Chief Pilot, both at Northrop to get their opinion about the speech she was writing. She asked Mike Kennedy about the early years and got input from the historian, Peter Merlin. This all started soon after we had been notified that I was going to be the recipient of the Walk of Honor Award.

Someone at Northrop faxed the actual Flight Test Report of the Tacit Blue Program to her and so much more information was gleaned from that document that helped her write her speech. In the months following, she began to read the speech to me every night before I went to bed. This reading continued until the night before the actual banquet. I tried to tell her several times I didn't think I could give the speech and finally in my state of dementia I did realize that she was going to give it. Each night as she read the speech to me and finished with her poem that she had written for me the Christmas of 1998, tears would come to my eyes and both of us would end up crying. She told me the night before the banquet that we absolutely could not cry at the banquet or she would loose her composure.

So I would sit watching her read or tell this beautiful story she had written about me every night for two months. Since I could only see from my right side. My wheelchair would be parked as close to the end of the couch as possible as she sat to my right. From there I could hear her and see her. Finally, the day came we all had been waiting for. The city had made special arrangements for me since I was disabled.

The City of Lancaster Walk of Honor begins with a late morning street fair each year. During this celebration, the honorees are presented to the general public. Keepsake posters giving a thumbnail description of the pilot's career and a picture are free. The honorees are available then for pictures and autographs to the crowd. Then during the evening festivities the atmosphere changes, guests and honorees are requested to wear formal attire, or Black Tie.

The following pictures show the granite monument with the five bronze placards; each year five are honored. Our two daughters and granddaughter, Heather, Velvet, and Alexandra were there with us. Our son was in the hospital at the time. My plaque is to the right of me in the picture. The next picture was taken of Cynda and me in our formal gear just prior to the banquet.

Since I was unable to be served dinner in the banquet hall, my caretaker served it in my room. It was later than my usual bed time and I had not had my bedtime medicine, so when Cynda came to check on me at the room she found I was having chills and a terrible headache. She gave me a couple of Advil and left for the ballroom. I stayed in bed fully dressed in our hotel room until time for the presentations. Then my caretaker for the evening wrapped me with a blanket over my tux and wheeled me to the convention center. I guess the Lord was with me, because not having my bedtime meds and getting the Advil kept me awake and alert for Cynda's presentation.

Cynda had requested to be first on the program since we didn't know how long it might last and I would not be able to sit there for long. Roy Martin and one of the City officials pushed me up on the stage and I sat in my wheelchair close to her left side. That way I could see her and hear her as she made her presentation. She was ready, nervous but confident and here is her speech for that night…the Walk of Honor…

(AFTER GETTING HERSELF TO THE PODIUM SHE LOOKED AT ME AND SMILED, THEN TO THE AUDIENCE OF 400, SHE SAID, "YOU'RE A VERY SCARY BUNCH!" A PAUSE FOLLOWED AS SHE FOUND HER COMPOSURE.)

(She announced the following statement before starting her speech)

On June 5th, 1948, No. 2 YB-49, piloted by Captain Glen Edwards departed stable flight and crashed in the desert near the Muroc test facility, thus ending Jack Northrop's dream of producing a flying wing aircraft. This led to the renaming of Muroc Air Force Base to Edwards Air Force Base.

On February 5th, 1982, a truly revolutionary aircraft known only as Tacit Blue, piloted by Northrop Test Pilot, Dick Thomas, successfully completed its maiden flight. The precursor for the B-2, Tacit Blue proved that Jack Northrop had the 'right stuff' after all!

GOOD EVENING LADIES AND GENTLEMEN:

Today has been very emotional for the Thomas family. Even though Dick can't express it, I know he is grateful for his peers' recognition of his accomplishments. But now, it is too late for him to stand up here and acknowledge this honor or enjoy the fruits of his labor of love.

So, I would like to speak to you from my heart.

In 1996 Dick announced at the dinner table that the family would know the next day what he had done in the black world. Well, that very evening on television, we saw a picture of the Tacit Blue. We never knew until the rest of the world knew.

For those of you who know Dick, you know he was not one to brag. To quote Mike Kennedy, a friend of forty years, Dick was never one to blow his own horn. Even though the Tacit Blue was declassified…Dick still never said much about the program to me.

Tacit Blue had its grand roll out at the Air Force Museum at Wright-Patterson Air Force Base, Ohio, May 22, 1996. From that moment on our family began to realize the significance of Tacit Blue.

Tacit Blue was one of the most successful technology demonstrator programs in Air Force history, meeting all program objectives and most low observable and sensor performance goals.

The following are excerpts from the Northrop Tacit Blue Flight Test Program Report:

Richard Thomas was intimately involved in all phases of the Tacit Blue program as the premier Northrop Chief Test Pilot. He was involved from the initial design phase, he flew the first four flights, he flew the final flight and over 70 of the total 135 flights; and he helped write the final report on the program. (Note: Keith Benson, who was the final Quality Assurance Mgr, told me there were only 135 flights even though 136 flights were designated. But all program objectives were met or exceeded early!)

Dick was directly involved in all phases of flight control systems with a 'What If' process. That if he or flight test engineering thought a failure could occur; it was discussed and thoroughly tested in the laboratory even if the design engineer insisted that the failure could not occur in his system. This was a brute force method to accomplish system engineering but was highly successful.

While simulator testing, Dick developed a philosophy of flying with the pilot in 'high gain'. This stressed the flight control system to the maximum and was frustrating for the FCS engineers. It required them to develop the FCS to state that it would continue to 'keep the blunt end forward' regardless of the rate of pilot input. During the test program the ability of the FCS to 'Keep the blunt end forward' was inadvertently tested by some of the less informed pilots. If Dick had not stressed the FCS in its early testing, these incidents could have resulted in the loss of the aircraft.

Due to the unstable nature of the aircraft, the flight control system was critical to the survival of the aircraft and the pilot. Every possible failure mode and combinations of failures was documented, analyzed and tested in the flight control test bench. Dick spent many long hours into late evenings going through all these failures and their consequences.

Dick participated in hangar flying the aircraft during the entire test program. Every failure, anomaly, curiosity, whatever, was analyzed for trend information, seriousness, and future system changes or corrective actions that may be required.

It was not luck that provided an aircraft for the Air Force Museum, but hard work and attention to detail by the entire test team. The key player that had the corporate knowledge and the skill to ensure a safe recovery of the aircraft, no matter what happened, was Dick Thomas.

During simulator and FCS test bench testing, the aircraft departed controlled flight in all directions, pitch up, pitch down, yawing and tumbling! Dick started keeping a yellow note pad that he used to list all the ways he could 'KILL HIMSELF' if something went wrong during the test program. This was truly a high risk flight test program accomplished over a period of three years with no serious incidents or accidents.

Dick's expertise as a pilot was demonstrated on numerous occasions. It was mandatory for the ground control room to be operational and monitor all Tacit Blue flights. One thing not tested prior to first flight was the coaxial switch. That one component failed on first flight take-off and Dick was completely on his own without any system health information and very little failure information available to him. The test conductor simply said 'Dick when you are comfortable with how it handles, you are cleared to come back and land!'

(Dick told me they said abort, abort, but he was too far down the runway and too high and I've learned from Lee Phillips, the first Quality Assurance Mgr. that Dick was experiencing severe pitch control problems, but as he overcame them, he flew a 25 minute first flight and then came back and landed. Lee was the last person to see him before he took off and the first person to congratulate him when he landed.) Lee also told me that during those first four flights, Dick and engineering worked out a

number of dangerous engineering problems making it safer for the next pilots to fly Tacit Blue.

During landing on a subsequent flight, water puddles had formed on the runway and when Tacit Blue rolled through the first large puddle the tires hydroplaned and the right main tire blew out as it exited the puddle. Dick was able to immediately apply nose wheel steering, opposite braking, and rudder to keep the aircraft from completely going off the runway. Without his immediate corrective action, Tacit Blue would have departed the runway and could have suffered extensive damage or even complete destruction.

In the historian, Peter Merlin's words, "Dick would be too humble to tell you about his achievements."

But I have learned much about my husband's work from the Flight Test Report and the men who worked with him. So I felt compelled to take this opportunity to share it with you.

Thanks go to Bob Wulf, retired Northrop V.P. of Engineering and Technology on Tacit Blue and the B-2 Bomber for this statement: 'Even though Tacit Blue no longer flies, the technology that it demonstrated lives on in the B-2 Bomber for low observables, shaping and materials, propulsion installation, electronic systems, flight controls and much more. Many elements are also evident in further developments since the mid 1980's including the F-22, F-35, Global Hawk and other unmanned aircraft, J-UCAS and…who knows what else is flying today like Tacit Blue was over 20 years ago to pave the way of the future'.

I found a yellow note pad with comments on Tacit Blue written by Dick in 2000:

"Recollections of Tacit Blue, was Tacit Blue unique or just normal evolution advancing through the technological jungle. I like to think of the results as the answer to required performance brought about by innovative designers as a normal evolution. The proof of the design in this industry is validated by the prolification of the concept throughout industry. After eighteen years every design proposal incorporates some form of the Tacit Blue concept. THIS IS VALIDATION OF CONCEPT."

…And so the ugly duckling metamorphosed into a beautiful swan, after all. (From the Tacit Blue to the B-2)

On September 25, 1974 Dick Flew the first flight on a new model F-5F, a two-seat prototype version of Northrop's F-5E international fighter, three feet longer and slightly heavier. I remember that morning rather well; all three kids were kept out of school so they could go to Edwards and watch the performance. We were watching by the runway and listening to the radio communications as Dick took to the sky. As he lifted off the runway, a slight problem occurred, and the nose dipped slightly. It gave us all a little scare but Dick was able to handle it and after a 43 minute flight landed safely at Edwards.

Subsequent flights identified unknowns related to high angle of attack and negative G flying qualities of the F-5E and F-5F. Dick was the test pilot that flew most of the hazardous high angle of attack flight tests and identified pilot procedures to recover from the out-of-control situations. Those spin recovery procedures established by Dick are still in use by fighter pilots all over the World.

Dick's love for his work took him far beyond his original dream. As his disease started to develop we had some soul searching moments—he told me that he thought he had flown more spin tests than any other test pilot—so Roy Martin who flew with Dick on the F-5F spin tests, researched and found 107 spin tests and over 600 maneuvers in the F-5E, F-5F and Sharknose F-5. I don't think that number included the Spanish C-101 where he performed the complete spin tests 'without' a recovery chute.

Dick was diagnosed with Parkinson's disease in 1996. In 1998 he was operated on for prostate cancer two weeks before his retirement party. The radiation seemed to accelerate the Parkinson's disease and Northrop put him on extended sick leave for two years. Consequently he was formally retired in November, 2000, at the age of 70.

Dick didn't do this job for glory or fame. He did it because he loved it more than anything else in the World. That probably speaks for many of you here tonight.

His mind is back in the sky now a lot of the time and he would love to be back in his childhood home in Mayville, New York. I think this poem I wrote for him Christmas 1998 says it all. I called it.....

I GAVE IT ALL!

I gave it all; just the shell is left.
I gave it all; I was one of the best.
Flight suit, helmet, flight card for spins,
Climb in the cockpit, strap me in.
Feel the excitement churning in my gut
Ready for that jet blast to take me up.
Give it the power and look towards the sky
Heart pumping fast for the wave-off bye.
Listen for the tower to call my sign
Hoping God is with me one more time.
Love is a feeling you never can explain
It can happen real fast when you're flying a plane.
It gets in your blood like a bad disease
And you never give it up till you're deceased.
Over 8000 hours in a hundred differ'nt planes
My body's al ache'n and racked with pain.
My head and my hands are shak'n in vain,
My heart's worn out and my brain's insane.
I gave it all, my family and friends
My wife and kids had to make amends.
Spent any years flying high and fast.
I gave it all, but I'm home at last.
God only knows how it feels to fly
High and fast across a clear blue sky,
Up with the eagles, the clouds, above trees
Looking down from Heaven seeing earth and seas,
Painted deserts, snow capped mountains
Artists' pallets, none could capture.
Forever sailing on a jet's windstream, dream'n
This must be like Heaven's rapture.
I'll never know why I loved it so

Each time I flew God made me anew.
Now I am earthbound no more to sky-dance
But, I'd do it again, just give me the chance.

Written by Cynda Thomas, October, 1998 for Dick's Christmas present

With the speech concluded, Cynda was relieved and put her arm around me… no tears and gave me a kiss. She was rewarded by a very appreciative audience and complemented many times. Her deed was done and she could relax and enjoy the rest of the 'show'. As for me, my caretaker took me home and put me to bed. She stayed until Cynda got home later. I was fast asleep. There could be no celebrating for me, but at last my fellow test pilots had honored me and I was content to go now.

In the following weeks and months my dementia became worse, my nightmares became more realistic and some days I would ask Cynda, "where is Cynda?"

She would tell me she was Cynda and I would argue with her, "No, I mean the other Cynda."   (I guess I meant the *young* one).

Some days I told her, "I visited with Mom this morning and had a nice long talk." My mother had passed away in the 70's.

During the late spring months when the days were warm and sunny Cynda would put me outside or take me in the car while she did her shopping. I hardly ever spoke; it was very difficult to make sense. I didn't see clearly and I was nearly deaf. Inside I knew I couldn't survive much longer, and what was the point. Tears would often come to my eyes. Cynda would see them and then she would cry too.

Day after day I sat in the wheelchair, starring out of partially blind eyes. "I'm winding down and it is hard to know who I am, where I am or what age I am. Sometimes you just don't want to wake up to this old world; I thought I had fought the good fight. I believed I had made my mark in aviation. I couldn't contribute anything more and it was time to check out. Well as I said before, life was a *hell of a ride* and I was glad to have had *the time of my life*."

EPILOGUE

On June 19, 2006, we kissed our man goodbye, and let his soul escape his old crippled body. I wrote the following poem for his memorial brochure:

End over end I spin,
Falling thru God's space.
It doesn't matter where you land
As long as it's in His grace.
But Heaven can't wait you see,
This time He is calling me.
So look up to the sky
I'm there flying high.
I'm flying again
Forever my friend.
Yes, I'm flying again
Forever my friend.

Velvet and I were always harping about Iacono as we found he was teaching at a college in Mississippi. But one day in 2007 this whole episode of Dr. Iacono was brought to a closure. Dick's friend, Bob Kaminski sent us a clipping from the L.A Times regarding Robert P. Iacono, the doctor who performed Dick's surgery and botched the job. Kaminski had been the witness I had asked to come and hear my confrontation with the doctor. It seems Iacono had flown his airplane, a

Beech Baron, into the Sandia Mountains in New Mexico and died in the crash on June 16, 2007, (almost a year to the day that our man expired June 19, 2006).

The ironic part of this story is, during those early courtship days, Dick had helped establish certification hours on the Beech TravelAir. Remember the story of taking me (Cynda) on dates to visit my brother in Oklahoma. The Beech TravelAir airplane was eventually reconfigured and renamed the *Beech Baron*! How's that for Karma?

◆   ◆   ◆

On a very sad day, October 8th, 2007, our son Richard G. Thomas II, passed away. He was only 46 years and had been suffering from an on-going illness for about ten years. He was a brilliant young man, who was an accomplished guitarist and had invented the Hercules Guitar Stand. Since he was not available for any of our family pictures I wanted to include him in his father's biography…he was his father's image.

◆   ◆   ◆

It has been two years now since Dick's departure to Higher Flight. Memories flood my mind of the good times we had and the ones we could have had…oh, too late. Sometimes in a flight suit, sometimes in a three-piece suit, he was always handsome, debonair and dashing. And as Dick strolled through those aerospace offices, he cut a swath that would turn any women's heart into a flutter! I wasn't blind to the challenges he and I faced. Early on a few 'married girlfriends' of mine gave him a smoldering look that would let him know they were available. But, test pilots were like rock stars or racecar drivers or any other celebrity that attracts attention to their 'manliness'. It happens even more if they have that 'silent sexy' look about them. He didn't seem to take advantage of their flirting; even though I'm sure it fed his huge 'ego'. But pilots' first love is their airplane!

Life was not always pleasant and wonderful with Dick. There were ups and downs as in any lifetime of marriage, moments of disappointment and lonely heartache. However I will remember and cherish all those special times we had together.

Living close to the Palmdale Plant 42 runway had its disadvantages, but it also had its advantages, for in past times the Lockheed Blackbird SR-71 or the 'Piggy-back 747-With the Space Shuttle' on its back would take off and fly very low over our area, leaving us breathless and thrilled.

Often now as I lay in bed unable to sleep, the late quiet night is sometimes disturbed as a U-2 screams into the black star-studded sky. One night I thought, *as I listened to the struggling vibrating thrust of the jet engine fading away in the night, how Dick would have loved to have been in the cockpit piercing the unknown night sky.*

Then one crisp early morning as I worked my front flower garden, the silence was suddenly broken when I heard a high pitched whine. Looking up I saw the culprit, the U-2 as it took off from the Palmdale facility at an 80 degree angle towards the sky. The pilot, a helmeted masked man in the cockpit, headed for a destination unknown to the world.

On that same day a few hours later a B-2 Bomber blasted off the identical runway with a thunderous roar. It banked to the north and went straight over our rooftop shaking our house and rattling the windows! Even after 45 years of watching the skies over the Antelope Valley…no matter where I am, the intrigue for me still controls my heart and constricts my throat. And each time I see that exotic B-2 Bomber fly over, I think that is part of Dick…his heart, his soul, his love. God's speed my love!

Printed in the United States
208724BV00003B/6/P